I0420340

# Becoming a Prepper
## How to Start Surviving Today

**By Bill Shepherd**

**© 2015**

All rights reserved. No part of this publication may be reproduced, distributed, or transmitted in any form or by any means, including photocopying, recording, or other electronic or mechanical methods, without the prior written permission of the publisher, except in the case of brief quotations embodied in critical reviews and certain other noncommercial uses permitted by copyright law.

**Are You Prepared? For almost anything? Or do you have no idea where to even start?**

Maybe you consider yourself an expert prepper already, but you don't have the basics down. Maybe you're just a complete beginner. No matter how long you've been prepping, we all make mistakes. It's natural. It's human. But there are ways you can learn from others and avoid the same mistakes that we all make, to get your prepping started off on the right foot. This book will help you get started in every category you need to jumpstart your prepping.

If you are interested in learning how to protect your family from any and all of the inevitable disasters that could potentially happen, this book is your first step to learning how to prepare for any emergency situation.

Don't wait - Get started today!

# Becoming a Prepper
## How to Start Surviving Today

There are numerous things that could occur that you need to be prepared for. Natural disasters, war, riots, economic collapse, chemical spills, fertilizer plant explosions and the ever-popular zombie apocalypse. Seriously, though, whatever the case may be, it helps to be prepared.

In this book, we'll go over ways to get your household ready for whatever is to come.

It is important to begin by evaluating exactly what the most likely risks are in your area and within your personal domestic situation, so you can focus your efforts better. Check websites for organizations in your area that will let you know which disasters are most likely to take place in that region.

"Bugging in" or sheltering in place is the most preferable option for most preppers. The thought of leaving a familiar spot with a limited amount of supplies and going headlong into the unknown is a scary proposition for many.

Of course, there may be a situation where you will have to leave due to a natural disaster, train derailment or chemical plant meltdown, for example. Once the lawman knocks on your door and tells you that it is time to go, you have little choice in the matter but to get out. You'll have to grab important paperwork and supplies and head to an alternate location.

Be careful not to go out and spend a lot of money on emergency supplies all at one time. This can be a real budget buster. There are subscription services that will ship supplies to your house a little at a time, and for a reasonable cost. This is helpful especially in the case of food.

You'll be able to easily rotate the food items out as they get close to their expiration dates instead of having everything go bad at the same time. Build up your supplies over time and before long you will have all the things you need should things go horribly wrong.

## Water

Water has a higher priority ranking than food, because you can exist for longer amount of time without food (about three weeks) than you can without water (about three days – and that's pushing it!) Many different aspects of water will be covered in this section, from collecting and storing to purifying and recycling.

Storing drinking water can be tricky. It, much like food, needs to be rotated out of your emergency supplies storage areas on a regular basis, usually every six months.

Barrels and 55-gallon drums need to be of food grade material. You will notice that many of these are made from blue polyethylene. That particular color restricts light and helps prevent algae growth.

Stainless steel tanks work well for water storage, but you might not be able to treat the water with chlorine, as it can corrode the steel. Look for tanks that have been specially coated so that this does not happen.

There are large, round, above ground storage tanks in colors like black, dark green, dark grey and dark brown for outdoor use. These are made from food grade BPA-Free polyethylene and they have built-in UV (ultraviolet) inhibitors to avoid color fading and breakdown from harsh sunlight. They are available in multiple sizes and can also be used for well water storage systems and drip irrigation systems.

Underground cisterns for water storage can hold thousands of gallons of water. They can be built with concrete block, but a much less labor intensive option is simply purchasing a polyethylene cistern tank and having it buried in the ground and installed by a professional installer. The tanks are ribbed and can withstand pressure and weight from the soil.

Do not locate the tanks in areas where vehicles may drive over them, however. Your collecting pipes and related items will be underground as well with this method, so it is virtually invisible.

If you will be storing water in plastic containers, be sure to store it away from things like fuel and pesticides, as hydrocarbon vapors can penetrate plastic and contaminate your water supply. You may want to elevate your containers instead of placing them directly on concrete. Try setting them on a wooden pallet.

Keep a good mix of small and large storage containers full of water on hand. The smaller bottles are more portable and very handy in a bug out situation where you can just grab and go. They can also be stored easily under the beds in your home if space for emergency supplies is limited, which is usually the case.

Water that has been stored for a long time can be "refreshed" by pouring it back and forth between two containers. This allows some air to get back in it and the process should improve the taste. Water should ideally be rotated out of your stock on a regular basis.

Remember that you don't just need water for drinking. You need to make sure you have enough on hand for tasks such as cooking, bathing, washing clothes and dishes, flushing toilets and firefighting.

Intruders may try to burn you out of your home. It may be worth installing a rooftop sprinkler system, or another way to dispense water to prevent a house fire. Looters may try to lob a flaming object through your windows to start a fire, but if the windows are coated with safety film and/or bars, hurricane shutters and the like, that will not happen.

Hopefully they will move on to the next house, but there's a chance they might look for other ways to burn and loot your home, so have all your firefighting bases covered.

Collecting WaterBathtub liners that are available will allow you to fill your tub with water at the first sign of danger to use for bathing or washing clothes and dishes. Fill your tub liner with water immediately, because if you wait too long, all that may be coming out of the tap is water that has been contaminated.

FEMA (Federal Emergency Management Agency) recommends shutting off the valve that supplies municipal water to your home in the event of a disaster. That way, polluted water from water purification stations which are no longer operating due to the emergency, cannot make its way into your home.

There will still be some good water still in your pipes. To retrieve this water that is standing in your pipes, there is a simple procedure you can follow. After you have shut off the main water valve to your home, put a container under the lowest faucet in your house and turn on the cold-water side.

Next, turn on a second faucet. This should allow air to enter the system and let you collect all the cold water from your pipes.

There are freestanding units for sale that pull water from the moisture in the air in your home. They can be pricey, but there are how-to videos on line with instructions on how to make one from a dehumidifier and a water filtration system.

Your hot water heater tank is also a source of emergency water. To retrieve the supply of water from your water heater, first shut off the breaker supplying electricity to it right at the breaker panel. Switch it from "On" to "Off" so that the heating element inside the water tank does not burn up when the tank is dry.

If you have a natural gas or propane water heater, shut it off according to the directions. If you have a tankless water heater, skip to the next section, as you will not be able to get water, because there is no tank.

Do you have a water softener? If so, the water might not be safe, especially for those with high blood pressure or cardiovascular or kidney disease due to the elevated levels of sodium from the water softener treatment. If you do not have this type of equipment installed, you can proceed to use the water for drinking or other purposes.

Turn off the water supply to the hot water heater by turning the ball valve (usually a flat lever with a colored handle) ¼ turn. If you have a gate valve, it will require a few turns to cut the supply of water off. Give the water in the tank time to cool off.

You do not want to collect scalding hot water out of the tank!

Locate the valve near the bottom of the tank. It should be threaded so that you can hook up a length of garden hose to it. Make sure the valve is clean.

Since it is located close to the floor, it most likely has some dirt on it. Connect a short length of clean hose to it and open the valve briefly in order to flush any debris out that may have collected in it. To get water out of the tank, you must first introduce air into the tank. Accomplish this by opening a hot water tap in the kitchen or in a bathroom. If you hear a sucking sound, that is perfectly normal and that means the procedure is working.

Collect the water that comes out of the hot water heater tank's valve into a clean container. You may see some sediment, which usually collects in the bottom of the tank, since it is heavier than water.

If this happens, just let the water sit in the bottom of the collection container until the sediment settles to the bottom. See the section of this report on purifying water if you plan on using the water from the hot water heater tank for drinking.

Shut the valve and allow the water heater to fill back up before switching the power to it back on, otherwise you could burn up the heating element. To refill the tank, open the supply valve back up and wait for the water to run out of the open hot water faucet.

Rainwater catchment systems allow you to harvest rainwater

from what falls on your rooftop. There is a diverter in the downspout attached to the rain gutters that switches positions once a certain amount of rain has already fallen on the roof. That way, you're not allowing dirt from the roof to get into the water storage tanks. Some people simply have a rain barrel with a screen to keep debris and insects out under each downspout.

Others have elaborate collection systems of metal or wooden racks with 55-gallon drums that are on their sides and linked to the other drums with pipe so that if one drum becomes filled, the water will flow to the next one in line, and so on. Either way, you can have at least some sort of rainwater collection setup to harvest the free water from the sky.

Please note that certain jurisdictions have rules and laws in place about collecting rainwater, so be sure to check with your locality for any information that may apply to rainwater harvesting. Harvested rainwater will need to be sanitized and filtered prior to consumption.

**Heating water**
Besides the obvious boiling water over a fire or on a stove, there are some off grid ways to accomplish this task.

If you coil up a hose within a pile of compost, it will warm your water. A low pile shaped like a rectangle with sides that slope was found to be able to register temperatures of 130 degrees Fahrenheit during the four-month life cycle of the pile. Heat from a compost pile is produced as a by-product of the microbial breakdown of organic material.

Composting is beneficial and easy to do with either a barrel or a bin type setup. The nutrient-rich soil that is a result of all those banana peels, eggshells and coffee grounds is wonderful for use in vegetable gardens.

Solar water heaters are available on the market and there are numerous on line videos where you can find out how to build one yourself. They are mounted on rooftops or walls that face the sun and the solar panels heat the fluid that is either pumped (in an active system) or flows via natural convection (in a passive system).

**Recycling water**
There are innovative sinks on the market, which attach to the top of the toilet tank, or replace it altogether. It takes the water you wash your hands with and sends it into the toilet tank. This water, known as greywater is then used for flushing the toilet. This is a great way to both recycle and conserve water.

Water from showers and the rinse cycle in the washing machine can be collected and reused with the implementation of a greywater system. Reusing your greywater keeps it out of the sewer or septic system, reducing the chance that it will pollute local bodies of water.

This reused water can be used for drip irrigation in landscaping applications. It can be used in vegetable gardens only if it does not come in contact with the edible part of the plant.

**Filtering water**
Purchase a water filter, like a five-stage filter pitcher for

instance and several personal-sized ones too. Those are very well suited for bug out bags and such. Make sure they are BPA (Bisphenol-A) free since that chemical, found in many plastics and in the liners of canned goods, can be unhealthy. Some do it yourself instructions can be found on line for making a water filtration unit out of ceramic filters, food grade buckets and a spigot.

**Purifying water**
Boiling water will kill organisms, but it will not remove harmful metals or chemicals.

There are iodine-based disinfection products that last longer than the popular water purification tablets. Too much iodine can be harmful, so do not use this method of purification for extended periods of time.

Sodium Chlorite / Chlorine Dioxide tablets. The sodium chlorite will generate chlorine dioxide enabling it to treat water. Chlorine destroys the cell walls of the bacterium, killing the organism. This method of water purification is used by municipalities all over the world.

You may have seen on TV the survivalist type reality shows. The episodes filmed in the desert locations have shown how solar stills are used for both collecting water and purifying water. The process involves digging a pit in the ground, and a smaller one in the very center to make an indent for the collection container.

Place a cup, bowl or other dish in the middle of the hole to hold the water that will be dripping into it, then place a large square of plastic sheeting material on top of the hole, using the dirt and rocks you dug out of the hole to help hold down the plastic sheeting.

Make sure there are no places around the edges where moisture can escape. Place a small rock in the center over the cup. The condensation from the underside of the plastic will drip into the container and you will have purified water.

## Food

Once the power goes out, you'd naturally work to consume any items in the refrigerator before they go bad. There is only a small window of time here before food spoils and is no longer safe to eat.

If the power is still out, the food in the freezer will still be good for a while. It will cook quickly as it probably has had a chance to thaw out a little bit. If the power still hasn't come back on, there are always the food supplies you stocked up on in the pantry and wherever you keep your emergency food supplies.

Probably the most common are good old canned goods. You will want to buy cans of food that you actually like and will eat. You can buy just about anything in a can these days. Compile a good collection of soups, chili, vegetables, fruit and more and remember to pick up a hand-operated can opener, if you don't already have one. Many canned goods are outfitted with pull-tabs, but that is not always the case. You may need to get in to that can and you won't be able to if the power is out.

Rice, beans, flour, wheat and other such staples can be bought by the 5-gallon bucket full to add to your stockpile. You will also want to procure things like cooking oil, condiments, spices and such. More information on this can be found in the checklist section of this report.

There are also MRE's (meal, ready to eat), which have been used by the military for decades. They are compact, easy to store, have a relatively long shelf life and are generally very tasty. You get a hot meal thanks to the included Flameless Ration Heater, a water-activated exothermic reaction product that emits heat.

Also typically included in the package are an entree, a side dish, a dessert, crackers or bread, a portion of either cheese, peanut butter or jelly, a utensil, a powdered beverage with a bag to mix it in, and an accessory pack with matches, a napkin, some gum and seasonings like salt and pepper. You can buy them by the case or individually. They are best stored in a cool, dry place.

Another option is freeze dried foods. These flash-frozen goodies have an incredibly long shelf life. Manufacturers of freeze-dried foods are often at gun shows offering samples of their products. They are actually pretty tasty and they do not take that long to rehydrate.

Dehydrated foods have had their water removed. Examples of these are fruits and vegetables, pasta, baking mixes, cereals, powdered eggs and powdered milk. You can purchase a food dehydrator and make and package this food yourself at home. The advantages are that the water is not there, but the vitamins and nutrients still are and dehydrated food takes up a lot less storage space than bulky cans.

In stockpiling food, think of **where** to store it. A sturdy shelving unit, a chest freezer, behind a false wall in the pantry, or scattered throughout the house if space is tight. You may even opt for building supplies of non-perishable food in several locations, such as an underground bunker, your basement, at an alternate bug-out location, and/or in a climate controlled rented storage unit.

Putting "all your eggs in one basket" might not be a good option. What if your food storage location burned in a fire? What if you were to get looted?

Make and keep an inventory of what foods you have on hand. This is one thing that preppers often forget to do.

An aquaponic system is a good thing to have at your home to provide food. It ensures an endless supply of vegetables and fish. The fertilizer from the fish tank located at the bottom of the system gets pumped up into a grow bed where vegetables are planted. These systems can be purchased in a kit and assembled, or you can buy a book and/or watch instructional videos on how to set up a system yourself.

The supplies you will need include a tank for the fish, like a barrel or a stock tank, a grow bed for the plants placed on a solid foundation, air and water pumps, media such as gravel for the grow beds, a bell siphon and various plumbing parts and supplies.

Aquaponics systems are usually built inside greenhouses but your local climate will help dictate what type of enclosure will work best. There are forums on line where you can ask questions of people who are experienced in setting up and maintaining these systems.

Fish that can be used successfully in aquaponics systems are tilapia, trout, carp, catfish and largemouth bass. Goldfish are good at producing waste, but are not recommended for eating, so this option may be ideal for any preppers who are vegan.

If you purchase the fish as fry, they will take longer to grow and won't produce enough fertilizer to support the grow beds. If you buy them as fingerlings, they are a little more expensive, but you will be one step closer to starting the vegetable growing process.

You'll want to start by growing kale, lettuce and other leafy vegetables as well as mint, basil and the like. Experiment and learn what grows best in your particular system and what you like to grow. You'll need to monitor and correct the pH (acidity and alkalinity) levels or the system will not operate to its greatest potential.

It may even fail. Plants in an aquaponics system generally prefer a slightly acidic pH and the fish and bacteria prefer a slightly alkaline pH. The ideal pH is somewhere between 6.8 and 7.

Later on, when your system is more established, you should be able to grow vegetables like cabbage, squash, peas, tomatoes, beans, broccoli, cauliflower, cucumbers and peppers.

To have seeds on hand to plant in the future, invest in an heirloom seed bank. These seed vaults last for many years and will ensure that you can grow healthy food should a crisis occur. These seeds have been saved and grown for multiple generations. They are open-pollinated, by either insects or wind without human intervention.

**How** you store food is just as important as what you are storing. Time, temperature, moisture, oxygen, light, and pests are the food storage concerns. The time issue can be solved by keeping track of your stock and rotating it out of your stockpile on a regular basis to keep everything fresh. Moisture, including things like high humidity is a major issue when trying to keep food stored. Use moisture-proof containers with good seals on them.

Also, do not place the containers directly on a concrete floor. Use some sort of a spacer in between. Oxygen can spoil food very quickly. You've seen it happen in your own refrigerator. If you store your food in a cool, dry area like a crawlspace, you most likely will not have to deal with the issue of temperature.

Oh, and burying your food storage containers is not a good option. How would you dig them up in the middle of winter, for instance? Pests can get into your food supply that way as well.

**Cooking**
The tried and true campfire will always be an option. If you are in an area where there are burn bans, be mindful of that before cooking at one in your backyard. Although, in extreme situations people must do what they have to do to survive. If you have a barbecue grill or a smoker outdoors, naturally you can always use those for cooking. Make sure the fuel supplies of propane, wood and charcoal are well-stocked.

A propane camping stove will allow you to cook food and boil water in the event that there is no power and you don't already have an alternate power source in place. There are portable kitchen type camp stoves that unfold to reveal a mini kitchen setup complete with burners, shelves and hooks for hanging utensils, pots and pans.

Many of these are reasonably priced and will be invaluable in the event of a crisis. They are compact for easy storage. One model even folds down into the size of a suitcase. This would be a great addition to the supplies in your bug-out vehicle, if you have one.

## Power

Solar, hydroelectric and wind are all alternate sources of power that you should study, explore, select and implement the one(s) that work best for your situation so it will be in place when the need arises. Solar power is very popular and panels have come way down in price.

There are also companies that will install the panels and allow you to make lease payments. That way you are not shelling out a lot of money all at once for a solar power setup. A major corporation produces roof shingles that have solar panels built in to them. These can be more aesthetically pleasing than multiple rows of panels on the rooftop.

Economical solar starter kits are readily available. You can start small and get acquainted with how solar power works. Then when you are more experienced with how it works and how you can apply it to your household needs, the kit can be expanded by adding more solar panels.

If you have a running stream or creek on your property and a drop in elevation, you might look in to a hydroelectric option to harness the power of the flowing water, converting kinetic energy into electrical energy. The way it works is water is sprayed with force against a compact water wheel. This can cause the wheel to spin with enough power to drive a generator or an alternator.

Using wind power involves erecting a tall windmill and this may not be the best option, depending on where you live. Windy locations that are at higher elevations are good candidates for this type of power generation, but you may run into issues with local zoning boards and homeowner association groups.

You might also invest in a good-sized portable generator. There are several on the market that are super quiet. That way you're not giving away your position to undesirables who may be looking to loot. Remember to shut off the main breaker in your house to prevent backfeed.

This is where the electrical current can reverse, go back through the circuit to the outside power grid, energize power lines or electrical systems in other buildings and bring great harm to utility or other workers. Generators must be used outdoors in a well-ventilated area to prevent carbon monoxide poisoning.

Follow the manufacturers instructions carefully! Portable generators run on gasoline and require oil to run as well, so be sure to have those items on hand.

Check with your local utility about having a generator standby switch installed at your breaker panel. Some will charge a monthly fee, which includes installation of the unit or give you the option of buying it outright with an additional charge for installation.

With this switch, you can control which appliances you want to use by flipping the breakers in your existing electric panel. No special wiring is needed for 100- or 200-amp residential electrical service.

This will allow you to use your portable generator without

having to run extension cords everywhere, which is a trip hazard and unsightly. You would just plug items into electrical outlets as you normally do.

A whole house or "standby" generator is another power source that can be used during disasters. You may have seen advertisements for these on television. They are installed outside your house much like an air conditioning unit and in the event of a power outage or a brownout, they come on within seconds when the automatic transfer switch signals the unit to start.

No refueling is needed as they run on propane or natural gas. Those two fuel sources may be hard to come by when things go horribly wrong, so keep that in mind.

# Heating

Unless you have a fireplace, wood stove, propane or oil heat, if disaster strikes and the power grid is affected, you'll have to find another way to heat your home. It's a good idea to have a backup for your primary heat source in any case.

You may have seen an item making the rounds on the Internet, which was supposedly a method for heating a dormitory room using votive candles, a bread pan and two flowerpots of different sizes. There is some debate on this as to whether it is a safe form of heating. One poster stated that the smaller (inner) flowerpot caught fire and flames quickly emerged out from under the stacked pots. It just goes to show that some forms of heating can be unsafe and must be used with caution.

Geothermal systems are clean and sustainable, but installation can be quite costly. They convert heat from the Earth into energy are constructed by drilling water or steam wells, similar to the process of drilling for oil. The heat that is extracted can also supply radiant heating to your flooring and hot water heater, in addition to supplying your home with nice warm air through the air ducts and vents.

A solar furnace can be built for about $50 from a dryer vent hose, black spray paint, wood and other easy-to-source materials. There are how-to videos on line to walk you through the process.

You might consider having an outdoor wood furnace installed to heat your home. This eliminates constantly having to bring messy firewood into the house. The unit is placed outside and gets connected to your existing ductwork. It can even be configured to heat your hot water heater as well as your garage or workshop. These units range in price from $1,000 to over $5,000 depending on size, capability and features. Be sure to factor in the installation costs as well.

Kerosene and propane heaters are another excellent source for home heating. Use caution and ensure a constant flow of fresh air to avoid carbon monoxide poisoning, which could easily result in death.

Make sure you have working carbon monoxide detectors in your home just in case. These are standard in new construction. Both types of heaters (kerosene and propane) come in different sizes. Propane "head" heaters are made to attach to the top of the tank or bottle and are lit by adjusting the knob and pressing a button. There are small tent sized heaters that just screw on to the top of a compact bottle of propane. Kerosene heaters need to be filled and the fuel is available at most gas stations. The fuel can even be treated with an additive to prolong its life.

## Cooling

Prepping your home with a viable cooling system can be a little trickier than heating it, as there are many more cost-effective options for heating than there are for cooling.

A geothermal system can cool your home in addition to heating it. Other options for cooling your home include a solar-powered air conditioners. These units are in the $3,000 range and work either on or off the grid.

If you do not have either of these cooling options available to you, there are some things you can do to keep cool when the power is out and you have no backup. Try dipping your bed sheets in cool water and wringing them out before you go to bed. The moisture will cool the air around you as the damp sheets evaporate. You can also hang these damp sheets in front of open windows at night when the air is a bit cooler.

Water misting systems commonly used on outdoor patios emit a very fine mist which cools the surrounding air by as much as 20 degrees. These units are commercially available and can also be constructed with supplies (nozzles, flexible tubing, valves, etc.) from your local hardware store.

Personal hand held battery operated misting fans have a water reservoir and you just squeeze the handle to spray the mist.

If your home has a basement, that is often your best bet for staying cool. When heat rises, cool air naturally collects on the lower levels.

Bucket air coolers or swamp coolers are readily available and relatively easy to construct yourself out of everyday materials including a five gallon bucket, water pump, SPST switches, a fan, dryer vent hose and a cigarette lighter plug. They operate on the principle of evaporative cooling and can run off a deep cycle marine battery, which is charged by a solar panel during the day.

Cooling towels placed on your head and neck, battery operated fans, kiddie pools filled with cool water and staying hydrated are more ways you can keep cool. Wearing light colored loose fitting clothing also helps.

## Air

You can only survive for three minutes without air. There may come a time where you might need to cover the air vents in your home due to a chemical spill or a quarantine situation. Cut plastic sheeting to size and affix with duct tape to windows, air vents and anything else that needs to be sealed up, like electrical outlets as air can even flow through them.

Gas masks can be used in the event of nuclear, biological or chemical warfare. Attacks will likely happen over large cities, so keep your location in mind when deciding whether or not to stock up on these supplies. They do not provide oxygen and will not help you in the event of a low-oxygen situation, such as a fire. If you decide to purchase gas masks, surplus ones are not a great choice, but given the current supply and demand, a surplus mask is better than no mask at all.

NBC (Nuclear, Biological and Chemical) type masks are the ones you should be looking for and spare filters are a must, so don't forget a set of those.
NIOSH (National Institute of Safety and Health) masks protect from airborne contaminants such as solvents, pesticides, and paint.

SCBA respirators are used by firefighters. Air is supplied by an attached carbon fiber wrapped tank, so you don't need to deal with replacing filters. The tanks usually last an hour or less, depending on how hard you are breathing.

SCBA masks are effective in protecting against higher concentrations of dangerous chemicals. The drawback is that they are heavy, weighing 30 pounds or more and specialized training is required to learn how to properly use and maintain them.

Reconsider any facial hair such as beards, as they may not allow a gas mask to fit properly, thereby rendering them virtually useless. Gas masks also are not made for and do not fit children.

**Air purifier**
Make sure to have certain houseplants on hand to keep the air in your house from becoming stale in an emergency situation when you are sheltering in, Plants like English Ivy, Boston Fern, Aloe Vera, Corn Cane and palms known as Lady, Bamboo and Areca will naturally cleanse the air and help remove toxins like formaldehyde and benzene. Use caution, as some plants are toxic to pets and small children.

## Defense

It might be best to keep your prepping plans on the down low, and not let people know about your survival preparations because when things get bad, the word will be out and folks will be lining up at your door for help. It is said that you should only confide in a few trusted individuals about your stockpile of supplies for when things go bad.

Another angle to this way of thinking involves those in your community and the skills that they can potentially bring to the table. They may have knowledge about prepping that you do not, and vice versa. It can pay to have a tight knit like-minded group who will be focused on survival and coming to the aid of their fellow men.

Do not underestimate people, however. Those with mental illness and guns as we have seen time and time again on the news are capable of causing great harm. There are also people high on drugs and their adrenaline is pumping at unprecedented rates.

You have all seen the police officer reality shows on TV where it takes a whole group of cops to be able to hold the intoxicated suspect down long enough to get the handcuffs on him or her. There are also the desperate and bold who will stop at nothing to get what they want and they often times have nothing to lose.

If it comes down to it, you will need to defend yourself and your home from these types of folks, and perhaps even roving gangs of intruders. They have either not stocked up on supplies, or they have run out of supplies, or their stockpile was ruined for whatever reason.

The latter may not pose much of a threat, because if they had enough foresight to acquire a stockpile of supplies, they are probably somewhat decent people, but desperate times call for desperate measures. In dire situations, they may try to gain entry into your home in any way possible. Calling 9-1-1 may not be an option, depending on the nature of the crisis.

You will want to set up a set of deterrents and then a defensible position outside of the home. Allowing the intruders to get all the way to the front door is not acceptable. A six-foot chain link fence around the perimeter of your property is a good start, especially if there is barbed wire at the top of it. If you live in a subdivision and are subject to homeowner's association CC&R's (covenants, conditions and restrictions) then consider using dense, thorny bushes like red raspberries or tall cactus around the perimeter of your property instead of a fence. If you are able to erect a fence, clear any objects from around it that would cause a disruption in your line of sight.

Battery powered LED (light emitting diode) motion sensor lights are another excellent deterrent. As soon as someone steps into the light's field of view, a bright spotlight comes on. This is also an indicator for you as far as knowing where activity is taking place, especially if you also have motion sensor alarms, such as a driveway alarm that emits a sound when an object breaks the beam between the sensors.

The alarm will sound and the lights will come on, pinpointing the exact location of a potential perimeter breach. If you have a security camera system installed, you will be alerted, as many camera systems have a motion sensor alarm built in. You will also be able to see on the monitor just what is occurring.

Speaking of seeing, **backup lighting** is an important component of sheltering in place. Candles come to mind at first. The problem is that they don't give off a whole lot of light. You would need to light many candles and if it is a hot, humid summer night, the last thing you want to do is add more heat to the home. Add some candles to your stash of supplies anyway. Just remember to use them with caution and never leave a candle unattended.

Flashlights are essential, so make sure you have plenty, along with a good supply of batteries. Headlamps are a great hands-free option. They are a combination flashlight and headband. There are LED lights that clip on to the brims of baseball caps so you can keep your hands free.

Solar garden lights are nice and all, but they are unfortunately not all that bright. They just wouldn't qualify as a good source for backup lighting in a crisis situation.

A solar flashlight might sound like an oxymoron, but such things really do exist. Charged by the power of the sun during the day, and providing bright light at night, solar flashlights are on the market, reasonably priced and some even come with an emergency battery backup. When they are not in use, you don't necessarily have to place them in the sun. They hold their charge for a very long time.

With all these lighting options available, be careful about how much light is noticeable at your residence. You'll read why in another section of this report.

It might be wise not to place "You Loot We Shoot" and other

similar type signs on your property as this type of evidence can be admissible in court should you be sued later by the intruders. People can (and often will) sue for anything at any time.

A well-trained protection dog is an asset - just don't advertise it. German Shepherds, Doberman Pinschers and Belgian Malinois dogs are excellent choices for this. As far as the signs, even a simple "Beware of Dog" sign could be used against you in court. One sign you might consider posting is a biohazard or quarantine sign.

People will most likely steer clear of your place if they think there are infectious diseases present. If there are complete anarchy conditions and there's little chance of a court battle, then a strongly worded sign warning people not to trespass on your property is probably warranted.

Other items with which to protect your home include weapons (firearms, blunt objects) door jammer security devices, clear safety window film, and blackout film for windows. If they see that you have power, they will think you also have resources. Don't be the nicest looking home on the block, either. That could make you a desirable target.

Scattering debris and broken glass around your home can act as a deterrent. If it looks as though your home has already been ransacked, the intruders are more likely to move on to the next one.

Once you have worked on your home to make it burglar-proof, give it the "chicken test" once over and attempt to break in to your own home, noting where the weak spots are and then go back and fix the deficiencies.

## Safe Room

This is a retreat to hole up in until help arrives. You need to remain there until your house has been cleared and you are completely safe. Designate a safe room also known as a panic room in your house to hide out in. Safe rooms ideally should include ventilation, thick reinforced walls and a bathroom.

If there is no adjoining bathroom, you can try using a line of products that let you place a complete bathroom just about anywhere, even where there is no plumbing. The system incorporates a macerator pump, which completely pulverizes all waste material into liquid form and then pumps it through a standard pipe into the septic or sewer system.

The safe room should be easily accessible from different areas of the house. There should be no windows to the outside - they are too easily breached. You can disguise the entrance to your safe room using a large mirror or a bookcase on hinges that swings open like a door. It could also be a trap door in the floor.

The actual door and doorframe to the safe room should be sturdy and made of reinforced material, and the door should swing inward and be secured with a quality, heavy-duty lock with a keypad. You don't want something that can be easily breached. Make sure you have an alert system that warns you of intruders and lets you know that it is time to move everyone to safety.

The alarm could be a dog, battery operated motion sensor alarms or other outdoor sensors that let you know someone has entered your property. There should be enough food, water and other supplies in the safe room to last at least 24 – 48 hours.

Remember to include such things as blankets and cold weather gear in case the power goes out, special medications for family members who require it, a first aid kit and hygiene products, especially if your safe room is not connected to a bathroom and all you have is a composting toilet, for instance.

Books and games like playing cards and board games can help pass the time. Its also a good idea to have a fire extinguisher, bulletproof vests and weapons with ammunition stored there as well, in the event that intruders attempt to burn your safe room down, and it comes down to a shootout.

Safe rooms need to be equipped with a method of summoning help, such as a cellphone, a landline phone which does not require electricity, a Ham or Citizens Band radio or a computer.

A system of security cameras will help you to determine if help has actually arrived, or if it is just the intruders trying to trick you into coming out. There are numerous products available like video doorbells that send live video to your cell phone and allow you to see and communicate with the person(s) at the door.

## Natural medicine

Create and build a kit of natural remedies. Nature has a way to heal every ailment and these treatments will come in handy in times of unrest when you can not get to a hospital, or the hospital is closed for whatever reason and there is no access to prescription medications.

Activated charcoal can be given in cases of diarrhea, ingestion of toxins or food poisoning.

Apple Cider Vinegar (raw, with "the mother") is unfiltered apple cider vinegar that can alleviate numerous maladies like acid reflux. It can be used on food – try it as a salad dressing - and you can drink a couple of tablespoons of it in a glass of water. Do not drink it straight as it can eventually damage your esophagus. It may help your body to maintain a state of alkalinity, which is important for good health.

Aloe Vera plant's leaves can be cut open and the gel inside can be used on skin burns. The plant also acts as a natural air purifier.

Baking soda is helpful for urinary tract infections when consumed orally.

Coconut Oil's fatty acids with medicinal properties makes it great to use in cooking instead of butter, as a body lotion, a hair conditioner, lip balm, massage oil, or mixed with salt to make a natural foot scrub. Those are just a few of about a hundred different uses for it. Just a tip, it melts at about 75 degrees Fahrenheit so if you open the jar and it is all liquid, do not be alarmed.

Tea Tree Oil is useful for adverse skin conditions. Dilute it with some water prior to application. It has a very strong, yet pleasant scent.

Arnica cream is useful for muscle injuries and bruises.

ClovesClove oil has healing properties and if you have tooth pain, try placing a whole clove in your mouth between the affected tooth and the inside of your cheek. The oil should help soothe the pain.

Turmeric contains curcumin, an anti-inflammatory. This is helpful if you are battling arthritis. It is a good idea to use this spice on your food while cooking.

Ginger helps with upset stomach and nausea.

St. John's Wort has been known to relieve mild to moderate depression and anxiety as effectively as many prescription drugs.

Neem oil can relieve dry skin and soothe skin that is itchy, red and irritated. It helps treat fungal infections, gingivitis and it is good for your head, helping to treat lice, dry scalp, dandruff and premature graying of the hair.

Garlic, fresh crushed offers cardiovascular and cancer-fighting benefits. The garlic extract capsules should provide benefits without the pungent odor.

Parsley has one of the highest levels of chlorophyll, which can help boost immunity, lower inflammation and clear toxins from the body.

Winter Green can be used in place of aspirin.

Magnolia flower is an effective herb for allergies and sinus conditions. Combined with other herbs, it can bring about temporary relief of nasal congestion, sneezing, itchiness and watery eyes. You can take the supplement by itself, in a tea or in formulations with other herbs.

Consult with your doctor and be sure your system is iodine sufficient. If your body contains enough iodine, this will usually help your system to fend off radiation poisoning in the case of a nuclear plant meltdown or other radioactive exposure situations.

## Bugging out

If you have to abandon your house for whatever reason, an alternate location can be as close as your own backyard. Underground bunkers are self-contained concealed shelters stocked with supplies and sturdy entry doors that are virtually impenetrable.

They range in size, anywhere from a small backyard bunker to a sizable decommissioned military missile launch site and can be as luxurious or as plain as you prefer. You and your family could retreat to one of these spaces and emerge when the all clear is given. The installation may require permits, so do your homework when considering one of these shelters. Hidden entrances are ideal so you can avoid detection by prying eyes.

You may be able to have space excavated under your garage, and the doorway can be right there on the garage floor. You may have to move your car to access the entrance.

**Bug Out Bag**

Say you're an expat living in a third-world country and there's a natural disaster, pandemic, civil unrest erupts or you are framed by unscrupulous individuals. When things get bad it is time to make an escape until things calm down. Make sure you have a bug-out bag ready so you can hit the road with supplies on hand. A large backpack filled with essential items would include:

A bag of survival tools
A sleeping bag
A bag of clothing
A hatchet
A trowel
A cooking set
A cup
A bowl
A spoon
A folding spatula
Hygiene supplies and toiletries
A towel
Swim goggles
A first aid kit
Sunscreen
A lightweight rain jacket or windbreaker
A hat
A handkerchief
A knife with a sharpening stone
A foil emergency blanket
Sandals
A Ham radio with antenna
A multi tool

Canned fuel
A slingshot with rounds
A solar lantern
A flashlight
A compass
25' rope
Earplugs
Food
Water

## Bug out vehicle

As with the bug out bag, circumstances in which you would leave your dwelling would have to be pretty severe. It is almost always better to shelter in place until things settle down. If you must leave though, to go provide assistance to someone perhaps, then a bug out vehicle is the way to travel.

Ideally a four-wheel drive, reliable, armored, rugged, solid urban escape vehicle which you can stock with supplies such as a portable camping kitchen (see "Cooking" section elsewhere in this report), extra clothing and bedding, pet food, leashes and any medications or other supplies your animals need,
Run-flat style tires would be ideal, as would a brush guard/push bumper, auxiliary gas tanks and enough room for your passengers and supplies.

There are numerous other vehicle options available, such as off/on window tint, a winch, night vision devices, a snorkel for crossing waterways, GPS, and communications equipment.

Dual sport motorcycles are another thing to consider as the 600cc models can travel faster than most cars, can be ridden on or off road and it is easy to navigate and weave through traffic jams on a bike. One drawback is that they are not well suited for inclement weather conditions. It is no fun riding a motorcycle in the rain, for one. If it is snowing, forget it. Perhaps a snowmobile is in order, in that case.

Close kin to the motorcycles are the side-by-side (UTV) utility vehicles. They have become quite popular over the past few years and are a good candidate for a bug out vehicle because they are powerful, rugged and good for on or off road traveling.

The stock side-by-side has plenty of options and accessories available like windshields, which you can apply bullet resistant film to, a trailer hitch for towing and even a roll bar mounted tent for the top of the vehicle! It will not collect sand, dirt and mud like a ground tent does. It sleeps two and there is a 2" high-density foam mattress, rain fly protected windows, mosquito netting and it is accessed easily by a telescoping aluminum ladder.

Boats can be driven to offshore locations to escape the turmoil on land. If you happen to set anchor in shark-infested waters, that is an added perimeter security bonus. You would still have to be on guard, naturally, and protect yourself from modern day pirates looking to board your vessel and rob you - or worse. You would need solar panels on the boat if you were to stay out on the water for any length of time, however.

The batteries would need to be kept charged in order to operate the bilge pumps and other important components. Also, depending on what size boat you have, you would need to return to shore and replenish your supplies.

Tiny houses constructed on dual axle trailers are all the rage these days. They free you from having too many belongings. There comes a time when you don't own your stuff – your stuff owns you! With a tiny house, you can bug out and take it all with you instead of leaving it behind. Tiny houses are ideal for off grid living and being that they are highly portable, this gives you the flexibility to relocate without having to "move" to a new house.

**Tips and Tricks**

Here are a few more tips for surviving a crisis situation.

Be healthy and in shape. When things turn chaotic, you'll need your wits about you and being agile and physically fit are of utmost importance. You may even want to become trained in some form of hand-to-hand combat such as karate as this could come in very handy.

Devise a plan with your family and hold regular fire drills. Develop a set of code words that can be used in certain situations, as well as evacuation plans, meeting locations, and assign tasks to those who are capable. Some examples of tasks include clearing the perimeter and night watch.

Purchase weapons for defense such as firearms and ammunition. Register for and take a handgun safety course if you haven't already. Practice shooting at local ranges to build solid marksman skills

Keep your important documents handy and ready to grab at a moment's notice in case you need to leave your home.

The amount of items geared towards prepping is immeasurable. There are a plethora of gadgets and supply items available and it can be difficult to choose what you might really need versus letting fear get the best of you and hoarding each and every prep-related item on the market.

Don't buy things that you do not know how to work. Can you read a compass? A sundial?

## CHECKLIST:

**Food – A minimum of 30 days worth, per person**

Canned vegetables, fruits and meats. Avoid buying cans that are dented.

Canned pineapple and tomato juices

Waxed hard cheeses

Rice – white

Pasta

Beans – pinto, kidney, lima, garbanzo

Black eyed peas

Flour - white, whole wheat

Hard red wheat

Cornmeal

Dry corn

Oats

Barley

Quinoa

Salt

Sugar

Honey - raw

Spices

Yeast

Baking Soda

Baking Powder

Powdered Milk

Vinegar

Coconut oil

Olive oil

Ghee

Coffee

Tea

Peanut Butter
Protein bars

Cooking equipment
Cast iron cookware

Cooking utensilscan opener (non-electric)
Disposable lighters and matches
Paper plates and cups
Forks, spoons, knives

## Water
At least one gallon of water, per person (and/or pet), per day
Bleach for purifying additional water if supplies run out
Coffee filters for removing any sediment prior to purifying water
Extra fuel for boiling water after you have used what is stored
Medicine dropper or measuring spoons for bleach     Water filters

## First Aid Kit
At least five pair of surgical gloves, medical grade
Forehead thermometer
Bandages: adhesive, butterfly, triangle, elastic and a pair of bandage scissors
Gauze pads: 2x2 and 4x4 sizes and a roll of gauze
Roll of cloth medical tape
Blood clotting solution
Ratchet strap tourniquets
Mylar survival blanket
Antiseptic wipes
Antibiotic ointment
Hand sanitizer

Plastic bag with resealable zipper closure
Saline solution
Safety Goggles
Tweezers
Tongue depressors
Permanent marker

**Toiletries**
Toilet paper
Feminine hygiene products
Cleansing wipes
Cotton balls
Cotton swabs
Soap
Shampoo and conditioner
Razors
Toothpaste
Sunscreen
Lip Balm
Calamine lotion
Camping shower – a 5-gallon capacity plastic bag with a showerhead, which can be heated by setting it out in the sun

Vodka – can be used for cooking or barter in addition to drinking. Has medicinal uses as well.

Sandbags – will help stop bullets and high water

Hand-crank radio and a battery powered radio. Both should be able to tune into weather radio stations.

Generator – portable, gasoline, oil, extension cords or a

generator standby switch, utility lights.

Construction supplies for repairs and maintenance.
Tools, tarps, plywood, nails, duct tape, pry bar, bolt cutters, work gloves, bungee cords, chainsaw, wrenches

High Quality non-GMO seeds for planting in a garden to grow food

A wall safe for cash and valuables.
It is a good idea to keep cash in different bank accounts. It is too easy for one account to get wiped out.
Money or items to barter. Foreign currency is good to have on hand.

Extra clothing and footwear for all types of weather.

Multiple flashlights with extra batteries and bulbs. In addition, purchase portable household battery solar chargers to keep all those flashlight and accessory batteries charged.

Pet Items – Food, water and food bowls, any medications, leashes

Keep inventory of all your gear and periodically go through it to make sure it is still in good working order, batteries are not corroded, etc.

If you address everything listed in this book, you will be well on your way to Being Prepared. You will know what you need to protect yourself and your loved ones. You will know how to survive. And, really, that's what prepping all about.

# SLADE: A SURVIVAL MEMOIR

When disaster struck, Slade Thompson chose to stay behind during the evacuations. Being a hobby prepper, he was certain he had enough supplies to last at least a year, besides, everyone would be back in a few weeks right?

Weeks have turned to months, and Slade is left with no idea why the people (and electricity) have failed to return. Dealing with his lack of supplies is quickly becoming an issue, and Slade is forced to venture out of the safety of his home in search of some.

What happens when he goes beyond the safe borders of his yard? Is he really as safe as he'd thought? How does Slade react when his neighborhood and home are threatened by raiders?

# Chapter 1

The sun shone brightly through the large bedroom window of the white rancher style home. The day was clear and sunny, warm, almost unseasonably so. As the sun rose in the sky it fell across the bed, and caused the occupant to stir.

Slade Thompson threw an arm over his eyes, shielding them from the bright light invading his room. He groaned, and for just a moment everything seemed normal. Perfectly, absolutely normal. He stretched lazily, as his slim, lightly muscled body adjusted to being awake.

For a moment he was perfectly content. It was like that feeling you get when you wake up just a little, and roll over, pulling the blankets with you. That deliciously sinful, indulgent feeling as you snuggle in to the warmth and comfort. He tried to cling to that feeling for just a moment more. Then he sat up, throwing the warm blankets to the end of the bed. He blinked at his surroundings as his mind caught up with him.

It had been weeks since he'd slept so long, so well, and his body was definitely thanking him for it. The late rising sun of autumn had been a welcome change, he thought. Slade glanced at his nightstand. It was a hand carved wooden affair that his grandfather had crafted for him 20 years ago. It was worn slightly with age, and the drawer had seen better days, but he'd never had the heart to get rid of it.

He reached over and plucked the digital watch from amid the items there. The watch itself was black plastic, with a compass encircling the face. The date and time, 8:15am, October 15$^{th}$ were displayed in black. Slade strapped the watch to his wrist as he had every morning. The first of his morning rituals.

The second was to pick up his phone. It was an older model he'd kept, one of the ones that still plugged into the wall. He picked it up and held it to his ear, holding his breath, and for the 120$^{th}$ day in a row, there was still no dial tone. He blew out the breath he'd been holding on a wistful sigh. He hadn't truly expected to hear that low beep, but he'd still hoped for just a moment.

Next was the crank radio. It was a neat little thing he'd stored in his basement for just such an occasion. He wound it quickly and easily, listening to the whir of the crank. Then, fiddling with the dial, he heard nothing but static.

He looked at his watch again. 8:17. He would try to find something for another 3 minutes and then give up, like every morning. Just every morning though, he still tried. It had been 100 days since it had stopped telling people to go to shelters. 100 days since the last time he'd heard another human voice. He was certain there must be others, maybe even in his neighborhood.

There's just something in our DNA that causes us to have an endless will and determination to find others. Because despite his relatively comfortable home, and easy life, he never stopped hoping that things would just go back to normal. At the very least, he hoped people would return and he could re-join humanity.

Sure, he'd considered searching out others from time to time, but there was just too much risk. He had everything he could need, and it was here. Leaving just seemed to be too big a gamble. Prepping had saved him much of the trouble he knew others would have faced. Most had fled to the shelters in the first weeks. On his street only a few like himself, had remained. Then the numbers dwindled as people lost hope for a quick resolution. He hadn't seen another human in 98 days.

Slade looked over at the bedside chair where his clothes were neatly folded, prepared the night before. He smirked, thinking that prior to all of this, he'd never been the kind of guy to be so anal about getting his clothes ready for the next day. In fact, his Go-bag had just had clothes crammed into it, rather than neatly folded.

While he'd been into prepping, he hadn't been totally serious about it. It had started out as a sort of hobby, and snow balled from there. If he was honest with himself, he'd never really expected any of this to happen. It had been a fun little exercise in preparedness. Just a what-if kind of thing. His friends had thought it was pretty funny, especially when he'd played up the Zombie Apocalypse angle.

Despite the fact he'd never been a truly, deeply, passionate Prepper, he'd done very well for himself. He thanked his lucky stars for the day that Mr. Andrews had introduced him to the survivalist life style.

He almost chuckled, remembering it all, but now wasn't the time for a trip down memory lane. He needed to start his day, he had to keep going, to stay busy or he knew he'd fall apart. Lack of human contact could do that to a person.

He hoped Andrews had made out okay in all this. The old guy was tough, and determined, but he'd been on his own, downright refused help. Slade tried to check in with him every so often, but was ever wary of looters. He didn't like to stray too far from his home. He realized that it had now been a few months since he'd seen him. He should probably check on him soon, though the old guy preferred little to no contact these days.

Slade shook his head, and climbed out of bed. He stretched again, and dropped to the floor. He began to do push-ups. His arms worked rapidly, lifting him up and down as he counted them out. Just a quick 20 to get his blood pumping in the morning. He had found it made him more alert. He quickly jumped to his feet and walked into his bathroom.

As he walked in the door, the strong scent of laundry detergent hit him, and he blinked a few times as he adjusted to it. On the sink there sat a can with just a little water left in it. Last he'd heard the water may have been contaminated, not that he had access to tap water anyway, what with the power being down. Instead he'd been rationing the canned water supply he'd had.

About a year ago, he'd scored an awesome deal on a 1-year supply of canned water for 1 person. Too bad he hadn't paid enough attention to realize it was a one year supply if you only used about 46 oz. a day, about 16 oz. short each day of the normally recommended amount. Being pretty sure that the situation hadn't been as grim as it had turned out to be, Slade hadn't started rationing it until recently. Now he had cut it down to attempt to stretch it out. He wasn't looking forward to the day he'd have to figure out how to purify more water.

He walked over to the sink and dipped his toothbrush into the water. He squeezed the nearly empty tube of toothpaste for all it was worth, and managed to get a dab. He'd have to dig the second to last one out for tonight. Slade brushed his teeth for a few minutes longer than he normally would have. He figured with no other dental care, he should be extra vigilant. Sometimes he wondered if the isolation had made him paranoid, and just a little too focused on the little details. Or maybe he was being smart. *Ha, who knows*, he thought, amused. He spit into the sink, and swished the little bit of water around his mouth before swallowing it.

Slade then stripped off his boxer-briefs and tossed them into the tub. The tub was filled with pale grey water. He'd collected rainwater to wash his clothes in, and periodically drained the tub and re-filled it with clean stuff. He grimaced at the dirty water and decided it was getting to be time to re-fill it. He dropped down beside the tub, and submerged his other clothes from the day before as well. He reached for the box of laundry soap flakes beside him, and sprinkled some into the well-used water. He didn't use much, but enough that when he mixed the water with his hand it bubbled a bit.

He let them sit while he got up and moved back to the sink. Slade reached over to grab the baby wipes off the back of the toilet. He pulled one out and used it to wipe up. Sure, it was nowhere near as good as an old-fashioned shower, or a bath, but it worked. It kept him clean (well, cleaner) and it kept him from smelling absolutely awful (though he certainly didn't smell like old spice anymore). He'd run out of deodorant over a month ago, and he tried to only use water for quick bathing every couple weeks or so, and only if he'd collected enough rain water for washing clothes, and to bathe. During the hot, dry summer that hadn't been as often as he would have liked.

After he finished washing up, he tossed the wipe into the trashcan, and turned his attention back to his clothes. He dropped back down to his knees and began to work on them. He scrubbed and kneaded each garment gently, trying not to damage them. He still had no idea when or if this would all be over, and it wasn't like a mall was nearby.

When he'd finished scrubbing each one, he rinsed it with as little water as possible. He kept a pitcher of rainwater by the tub, but he was always cautious not to use too much for fear he'd run out. Running out, now there was a thought that was ever present in his mind. It was a phrase that ran through it every time he used anything, ate or drank anything. Any of those activities these days sent his mind into a spiral of calculations that left him with a headache and a dismal outlook on the future.

After rinsing each item he twisted the water out of it, and hung it from the shower rack to dry in the sunlight from the large bathroom window.

Slade headed back to the bedroom and grabbed his clothes. A pair of once light blue, now dark grey boxer-briefs, a pair of well-worn jeans, and a red plaid shirt. He wasn't doing too bad in the clothes department. Yet, his mind seemed to pipe up sarcastically, he wasn't doing too bad yet. He was glad he hadn't been into the whole jeans with holes in them thing, because pretty shortly he would have had nothing left. Some of his older jeans even looked like those ones that were so fashionable these days. He laughed a little to himself.

"Got to keep your sense of humor, Slade," he said out loud. "And remember to talk out loud, keep the old voice limber."

Throwing on his clothes, he mused about the oddities of solitude. After the first few waves of evacuations were over, he was basically left alone with only a few other residents in the neighborhood, none of who were interested in being friendly with one another. At first Slade hadn't talked at all. Then he'd noticed that his voice was difficult to use if he hadn't spoken in a while. So he'd tried to, at least, talk out loud every so often. Sing to himself sometimes.

He was no Axle Rose, but he was pretty good he figured, and the only one listening was him anyway. Every so often he wondered; if he stopped talking altogether, would his vocal cords atrophy? Would he lose the ability to speak just from lack of use? He had no idea, but he wasn't about to find out the hard way. Slade Thompson was a lot of things, but martyr was not one of them. Not by a long shot.

"Okay, time to get some breakfast!" he said to himself.

Slade grinned. He walked out of his bedroom and down the hall. He didn't look at the walls. He didn't want to see the happy pictures of his parents and himself. He didn't want to see the pictures of his girlfriend. He preferred to keep his worrying about his loved ones confined to the night. When he could lie in the darkness and wonder about them. Where they were, what they were thinking and did they think he'd survived, or were they already convinced he'd died. But, really, it didn't matter if he looked or not, as the thoughts gnawed at him whenever he walked down the hallway. It was just expounded by the visual reminder.

He walked into the kitchen still feeling grim, and walked over to the cupboards. He flung open the door of one, and reached in, grabbing an MRE breakfast item out of it. MREs weren't too awful. A lot he even kind of liked. Peanut butter for example, was rather tasty. He was just glad he had food, especially since he'd run out of the 'real' stuff a long, long time ago.

He popped open the pouch and pulled out the strawberry toaster pastry and took a bite. Sure it was no iced pop tart, but it was good. Maybe it was because he was hungry, maybe it was because after a month he sometimes felt like he could barely remember food before MREs. Whatever it was, he actually enjoyed a lot of the MREs. After he finished his not-pop-tart, he decided it was time to get some exercise in.

"What to do, what to do?" he mused. "Maybe a little sword fighting?" A grin spread across his face. He couldn't help it: if ever he needed a laugh, today was it.

Walking into the living room, his mood brightened considerably. Today was going to be a good day, he told himself. He was going to start it by practicing sword fighting. In a manner of speaking...

Slade had felt pretty nerdy at first, when this had become a regular activity for him, but whatever made you laugh, and exercise was probably good for you. Whenever he did this, he imagined his friends laughing at him, and him laughing with them. It was good for him, good for his soul to feel connected to them despite the separation.

He walked to the couch and grabbed the light-saber from the bin next to it. It had been a gag gift from his friends after they'd all gone to see one of the movies together. He'd been the only one who had expressed a positive opinion about the movie, and his friends had found it hysterical. He'd thought he'd never live it down. Now it served as a reminder of the good times.

He raised the saber and swung it, thrust it, pretended to parry, and twirled it in his hands. In his mind, he pretended to have an epic fight. He could practically see his dark opponent as he played out a scene that existed only in his imagination.

After about an hour of this activity it was time for Slade to head downstairs and check on his supplies. It had become an almost obsessive-compulsive thing, checking the supplies. Although he was well prepared, and he knew it, he couldn't help checking every morning. He had to count and touch, and see it all, just to remind himself he would be okay.

Slade tossed the saber onto his couch and walked down the hall. He grabbed the flashlight on the countertop beside the basement door. He flicked it on, and opened the door, which creaked loudly.

"Someday I'll get around to oiling you," he told the door as he descended the stairs. More and more often, Slade had begun finding himself talking to inanimate objects. It was kind of comforting to talk to someone-- something, other than himself.

At the bottom of the stairs, the large unfinished basement was well organized. To his left was a palette with cans of water stacked in rows. He still had enough for 230 days. More if he cut down his intake a bit. Not knowing when things would return to normal, he'd been trying to ration it a bit. Not so much as to cause any physical or psychological symptoms, but not the optimal amount either.

When all this had started Slade had expected it to last a few weeks, then weeks had turned to months, and here he was. Still waiting for news about what had happened, and damn curious about why no one had returned.

Slade stepped to the right and examined each of the stacked boxes of MRE's. He'd not needed to reduce his intake since he'd managed to find a really good deal, and still had more than enough to make it to the end of the year. Next he checked on the one truly irrational fear he had: that some creature or critter would get into his food supply and decimate it. He knew that it was very unlikely, improbable even. Still, he checked each of the stacked boxes making sure no little critters had gotten into them. The last thing he wanted was to have his supplies decimated by mice or bugs.

Once he was satisfied there was no evidence of any sort of invasion, he moved on to the row of plastic drawers beside it. He opened the first drawer and looked in at the packs of batteries. He counted out the AAAs, AAs, C and D batteries.

With a sigh, he had to admit he didn't like the numbers. He was getting low on batteries. He'd already started trying to use them as little as possible, but he was going through his supply much faster than he'd calculated. He hadn't anticipated the total black out that had occurred. And certainly not on it lasting for months.

He slammed the drawer closed in frustration and opened the next one; books he'd read only once already. He'd run out of totally new ones a long time ago and books were probably one of the only things keeping him sane with all this free time he suddenly had. He was running dangerously low on them, about 3 more to be exact. He ran a hand through his hair: he was beginning to realize that, though these weren't necessities, they sure made life here a lot more bearable.

As he closed the drawer, a feeling akin to claustrophobia overcame him. He knew that books were just small things to be so worried over, but they were like his escape from the isolation. He could delve into other worlds and interact with characters, almost feel like he was somewhere other than his lonely little house in the empty neighborhood.

Moving on, he closed the drawer and headed to the shelving units on the far wall. Just with a quick glance he could tell he was running low on toilet paper. He'd never paid attention to just how much he'd used before, and he'd sorely underestimated how much a year's supply would be. He had just 2 packs of 24 double rolls left. He shook his head at himself.

"No doubt that was my dumbest mistake. I guess when you don't think it's really going to happen it's easy to overlook the small details," he told himself.

The next spot on the shelf was bare, and it was the one bothering him the most. It was the spot where he'd kept the Ibuprofen. His last bottle was upstairs in the medicine cabinet, and only a handful of pills were left. This was yet another mistake he'd made.

Before the disaster he'd never really had many headaches. Now he had at least one a day. He wondered if it was just a result of his limited intake of water, or if he'd been exposed to something. Only time would tell, and he wasn't going to worry about it when he had so many other things to worry about.

Looking around the room, he had to acknowledge that things were getting a bit desperate. Okay, so maybe desperate is an exaggeration, he admitted to himself, but it was about to become a hell of a lot less pleasant around here if he didn't take some steps to remedy the situation.

"It's time," he said. Yes, he thought, he would have to venture out for supplies.

# Chapter 2

Slade paced around his living room, thinking. If he were going to venture beyond his own backyard, he would need to be prepared. He was practically thinking like a boy scout nowadays, always be prepared and all that jazz.  If he was going to go out today, he really needed to get a move on. He'd need to load up his versi-pack, grab his go-bag, figure out what he needed to get and where to get it from.

There was the crux; where could he go for supplies? It was much too far to walk from his suburban sub-division to the nearest store and he wasn't sure how comfortable he was with the idea of looting his neighbor's homes. Slade had always been honest to a fault. He'd never be able to take things from these people. He knew them, and even if they might never come back, something about it felt... wrong.

Feeling kind of ridiculous he decided he would have to go at least a few streets away. To soothe his guilty conscience he'd leave a note with his number and that way if things ever did return to normal he could re-pay whoever he'd had to borrow from.

With that settled, Slade went to his office, and got out a notepad. Sitting down in front of his useless computer, he started his list. What would he need to bring with him? His go-bag had a few MRE's, a change of clothes, a rolled up sleeping bag, water, flashlight and batteries.

In his versi-pack he'd put a multi-tool, a mini pry-bar, the lock pick kit he'd gotten as a gag gift a few summers ago. Who knew it might actually come in handy. His friend, Joe, had gotten it for him after Slade had managed to lock himself out of his house twice times in a month. Para-cord could come in useful, so he'd bring some of that too. He'd also throw in his folding knife as a back up for the fixed blade he'd strap to his belt. If he owned a gun he'd bring that too.

Slade had never been gotten around to getting a gun. It was always on his list of things to do: buy a gun, and learn how to shoot. He'd just never managed to find time; he'd been too busy until it was too late. Oh well, the knives would have to do for self-defense.

Wracking his mind for anything else he might need, Slade gave a shrug. It was as prepared as he was going to get. Now he needed to think about what supplies he should collect. He divided up the remainder of the page into three columns: Need, Want and Luxury.

Under the need heading he wrote out things he truly needed: Batteries, possibly rechargeable ones, socks, a solar charger, canned/non-perishable food, medical supplies, Tylenol and Advil.

Beneath want he listed: Generator, Gas, Deodorant, a handheld game system, cards, and books.

Finally he listed the luxury items: Candy, model kits, chocolate bars.

Looking his list over Slade couldn't help but feel he was forgetting something. With another shrug to himself, he acknowledged that if he couldn't think of it now, he probably didn't need it. After one last run through of his list Slade set about collecting the items he'd listed and preparing himself for his first foray into the wide, wide world in a long time.

Once he'd finished gathering and packing everything he'd need Slade jogged back to his bedroom to change his clothes into something more suitable. He reached into his drawers and grabbed the black combat pants, black socks, white undershirt and a blue Hawaiian shirt he'd been saving for just this occasion. He smiled, remembering why he'd chosen the Hawaiian shirt for his excursion - He figured no one would shoot the guy who's there to play limbo! It's just friendly. Non-threatening, or at least it would seem that way, until he needed to be. He tossed the clothes onto the bed along with his belt. The pouch holding his fixed blade survival knife was threaded onto it.

Slade got dressed in a hurry, knowing if he was going to try to make it back before dark he'd need to hurry it up a bit. After he'd changed and grabbed his belt, he headed downstairs for his versi-pack, go-bag and combat boots.

He paused at the top of the stairs to take a deep breath as a feeling overcame him that he couldn't place. After a few seconds he realized it was a kind of anxiety, and he wondered if this was how agoraphobics felt? Nervous at the thought of leaving their homes. He shook himself out of it though, and climbed down the stairs.

Picking up his bags, and getting a duffle bag from his closet Slade went to the front door for his boots. He slipped them on, and zipped them up. He'd chosen a pair with a zipper on the inner side for their easy on/off feature. He wasn't the type to lace and unlace boots every time he took them off. He'd worn out more than one pair of boots that way.

Slade stood up and strapped his versi-pack to his belt, and then threaded it through his belt loops. A grim determination had begun to settle over him, and he was doing his best not to work himself up about what may lie beyond the safety of his home. If he thought like that for too long, he'd never manage to leave the house.

"Man up Slade!" he exclaimed to himself in a bit of frustration. He laughed nervously as he headed for the back door.

## Chapter 3

Stepping out into his backyard was liberating. The knowledge that he would be going beyond his own safe boundaries was both exciting and frightening. Slade turned his face up into the sun, and took a moment to take a clarifying deep breath. Once he felt steady, he looked around the neighborhood. It was pretty boring and predictable as sub-divisions went. Rows of duplexes, then rows of ranchers like his, then two-story's, and then duplexes again. All of the houses looked basically the same. Planned communities from the '80's tended to be pretty bland.

Slade had always liked it though. It was a comfortable, nice community, and he realized with a pang, that he really missed his neighbor's. The Johnsons and their dogs included. He'd never understand how a person could have so many dogs, and stay sane. But they were like babies to the Johnsons and each one was loved.

Slade walked next door, looking in the Aldershot's house. Greg and Marsha Aldershot had just had a baby before the disaster: little Sierra had only been a couple weeks old when the evacuations had started. He really hoped they were doing okay. He'd never met a couple more in love than they'd been. Totally content with their slice of suburbia, only to have it snatched away so soon after the birth of their first child.

He knew Greg would be totally fine with him taking whatever he needed, but he still felt guilty as he lifted up the mat in back, and found the spare key.

Unlocking the door, Greg, poked his head inside. He was positive Greg and Marsha had left in the first wave, but just in case he shouted out to them.

"Greg? Marsha? Anyone home?" He called loudly. Silence was his only answer and he slipped inside. He searched the kitchen first. He rooted through the cupboards, not much was good anymore. Marsha had been into organic food, so it seemed most had spoiled shortly after the evacuations.

He was just about to give up in the kitchen when he spotted a case of cola in a bottom cupboard.

"Score!" he said to himself. Cola would be a nice little treat, and he was excited to have found some. Before the disaster he'd been a soda addict. He'd had at least one can a day. That habit had long since died.

He turned his attention to the rest of the house and was elated to find a few things he could use. In the bathroom he'd found toilet paper and Tylenol. A nearly full bottle of it. He'd also found a first aid kit. He piled the new supplies up with his Cola. A pang of guilt hit him again as he realized he was stealing from new parents. With a sigh, he walked over to the fridge and scrawled a note on the white surface:

> Dear Greg and Marsha,
> Sorry I had to borrow
> some supplies from you.
> If this ever ends and you
> get to come home I owe
> you:

1 Case Cola
1 24 Pack Double Rolls
Toilet Paper
1 Bottle of Tylenol
1 First Aid Kit.
So sorry. Please forgive
me,
Slade from next door

With that done, Slade felt a bit of relief from his guilt. He gathered up his finds, and headed back to his place to drop them off before he ventured further away. Although he knew some of his neighbor's would have been fine with him taking their things, the amount of guilt he was feeling over the Aldershot's house was getting to him.

He knew it was a ridiculous sentiment. For all he knew his neighbors were never coming back. Hell, they could be dead. He certainly hoped they weren't though. Still, his next house would have to be quite a bit further away. He didn't want to be thinking himself in circles about the fate of his neighbors each time he borrowed something.

Looking up at the sun, which was lower in the sky than he would have liked, he decided that he would start at the next street over, instead of a few over. It was just too late in the day, and he really didn't want to be outside at night. Years of zombie flicks had made him a tad paranoid at night now that the streets were deserted. Not that there was a zombie apocalypse or anything, just that he would inevitably end up creeping himself out. The quiet was so eerie, especially in the dark.

Slade decided the best way to assuage his guilt for now would be to just make sure he only took a few things from each house. Then he wouldn't be cleaning anyone out, should they come back.

# Chapter 4

Slade crept between the rows of houses, and scurried across roads. Knowing what he was about to do was making him jumpy. He felt as though he was being watched, but shrugged it off as paranoia. He felt like a child about to do something his parents had warned him never to do. As though someone was waiting in the wings to shout 'A ha!" the moment he picked a house and tried gaining entrance. He shook himself out of it though. In all likelihood, there simply was no one left here to judge.

From the looks of the houses, and yards they'd been abandoned. Nothing around here looked as though it had been lived in for months. That was the truly creepy part; When Slade was in his own house it was easy to ignore the deserted homes around him. Easy to pretend that nothing was out of place. However, when confronted with reality like this, he couldn't help but notice the wrongness of it all.

The silence, the total lack of life, was getting to him the more time he spent out here. Slade decided to go one more street over to Inkwell. Inkwell Street was filled with larger three story homes. It was more of a luxury street than his own, and he suspected was probably better stocked. He was also fair certain that anyone living on Inkwell would have been on the first evacuation flights. People who were well off had no reason to stay, they could start over anywhere, he figured. And besides, it would give him a chance to drop in on Mr. Andrews when he was done.

He cut through another backyard, and jogged across the street. After sizing up the house in front of him, and looking around a few times to make sure no one was watching from the windows, Slade walked up the driveway. At the end of it, close to the garage, was a red minivan. It was a newer model, but it looked unused, with a layer of dusty grime coating it. Slade looked at the stick figure family on the back window. A mom, dad, and six kids smiled at him in various sporting outfits. Well, that seemed like the kind of house that definitely had snacks in it!

Slade felt a nervous knot in his stomach as he approached the house. He walked up the cobblestone walkway, and climbed the three grey cement steps to the blue wooden door. A silver and green ribbon wreath had fallen off its hook, and lay discarded near the front. Something about it hit Slade hard in the gut. Maybe it was the fact that this had once been a cherished family home, but now lay deserted? Maybe it was the obvious care, and love that had gone into the meticulous decoration of the home? Whatever it was, he was feeling a longing for normalcy that was almost overpowering.

He looked up at the big house, and admitted to himself, that perhaps staying had been the wrong choice. Perhaps he would have been better off following his parents and girlfriend in the evacuation. But, he'd made his choice, and regrets would get him nowhere. The sun was sinking ever lower in the sky, and he needed to do this.

Slade reached for the knob, and turned the handle. Yes! It was unlocked. Lots of people left their doors unlocked during evacuations to prevent emergency responders from breaking their doors in to do checks. These lovely people had obviously shared that thought, and Slade was infinitely glad they had. He wasn't sure he could even use his lock picking kit. The few times he'd tried it he'd been less than successful, though he'd never given it a truly serious attempt.

Slade slowly opened the door and stepped in, careful to avoid the wreath. He looked around at the layer of dust that had settled, and knew that no one was here. Still, better safe than sorry. He certainly didn't want to run into an armed and frightened occupant in one of these homes.

"Hello? Is anyone here? If there's anyone in here I just want you to know I'm only looking for supplies. I don't want to hurt anyone, and if you're home I'll just leave!" He called out, stumbling over his own words.

Really, what were you supposed to say to someone whose house you intended to loot? He flinched at his own thoughts, looting wasn't the right word for what he was dong was it? Looting was a crime of opportunity; it was greedy people stealing from stores during riots, or Nazi's stealing art during wartime. *What I'm doing is survival*, thought Slade, *not profiting from disaster*.

When no answer to his inquiry came, Slade walked farther into the home, listening carefully for any rustling that might indicate someone was there. He figured he should check all the rooms first, like the police did on TV, clear the place. He walked from room to room on the main floor, not finding anyone. Then he crept up the stairs and checked the bedrooms. 2 of the 5 bedrooms had bunk beds, Slade briefly wondered if they were twins. The, 3rd and 4th bedrooms clearly belonged to a teenage girl and boy.

The girl's room was covered in pink, with pictures plastered over her vanity mirror. Posters of Justin Bieber hung on the walls.

The boy's room was a pile of dirty clothes, and video game cases. A TV with an X-Box sat on his dresser, and the controller was tossed on the bed.

The last room was the master bedroom, it was empty as well, the large four-poster bed was still made, with a hand-made quilt laying over it. Slade was instantly reminded of his mother's room, and the quilt his Nana had made her. The one she'd lovingly repaired over the years, and had always told Slade she'd give to his daughter someday. His mom had always loved family heirlooms, and the idea of passing them down to her grandchildren. Thanks to the disaster she hadn't gotten any, maybe never would, Slade thought morosely.

He backed out of the room and decided to check the basement. He walked down the steps, and found the stairs to the basement. He pulled out his flashlight and flicked it on, descending the stairs as he did. A quick look around revealed some batteries in a desk drawer, which he pocketed. He also found a stack of old books in a box that looked like they'd been getting ready for a yard sale. He rifled through it and picked out a few, tossing them into his bag.

After he thoroughly searched the basement, he'd determined there was nothing else he could use. Slade decided he'd head upstairs and check the bedrooms again. Maybe one of the teens had a solar charger, or handheld game that had gotten left behind.

Luckily for Slade, he'd guessed right, and did find a solar charger and some batteries in the teen girls room. He put them in his bag, and went to check the other rooms. In the teen boy's room he found another few books that he borrowed, but nothing else.

A quick check of the other rooms didn't yield much, and he headed down to check the ground floor for supplies.

In the kitchen he found a few snack items that he grabbed immediately: A bag of Cheetos, a few cup-of-soup packets, and some Marshmallow Tammy's. He was pretty excited about the Tammy's; they were marshmallows covered in coconut and chocolate. One of his favorite treats from before.

He hadn't found everything on his list, by any means, but he'd gotten a few things. He figured one more house was all he had time for today, so he headed to the door, intending to go to the next house.

When Slade opened the front door he was met with a sound he hadn't heard in months. His heart began to race and his palms got sweaty as he placed the noise. It was the deep rumble of large vehicles. Trucks of some sort, anyway. He felt sick, and he swallowed hard. Who could it be? Rescuers? The military? People returning home? Or just someone like him? Maybe someone worse?

Whoever it was, Slade was going to keep his distance until he knew for sure what was going on. He closed the door, and sat down with his back against it, taking deep, gulping breaths as he tried to come up with a plan.

## Chapter 5

Jacob Andrews woke from his nap in his easy chair. He'd been startled awake by the sound of vehicles. "Finally!" he grumbled. It was a sound he hadn't heard in a very long time, and he was curious about just who was driving up *his* street. He tossed the weathered copy of Moby Dick from his chest onto the end table. It had been his third read through and it was getting rather tedious.

Jacob hefted himself out of the recliner, age making the process more difficult than it used to be. His joints groaned, protesting at the rapid movement they were no longer used to. He walked to the window as he rubbed the sleep from his eyes. He wanted to make certain it was the people returning home, and not the military. Jacob had never been a fan of the military; they were always trying to tell him what to do. He'd left the military over 40 years ago now, and was still a bit resentful that his 20 years of service had left him with a bad back, bad knees and one ear that didn't work quite right.

Jacob pulled back the curtain and smiled when he saw civilian trucks coming up the road. The smile was short lived, though, and faded once he noticed the men in the trucks. These were not his friends and neighbors. These were strangers. Possibly dangerous ones.

The men stopped at the end of the road and began to get out of their trucks. They were in hunting gear, and had assault rifles slung over their shoulders like proud trophies. Most of them were, big and tall, rough looking. Jacob frowned as they began walking up to houses and kicking in doors. Disappearing inside and coming out with whatever they could carry, loading it on the trucks.

Maybe they just needed supplies. Jacob knew there were people who hadn't been as prepared for the disaster as he was. Hell, his own son had thought he was crazy. A 'hoarder' he'd called him, but Jacob had denied it, and now he was reaping the rewards of his efforts.

Jacob hoped that these men were just pillaging to survive, hell, if he needed supplies he'd be out there gathering them too. Something about them was rubbing him the wrong way though, and he heard alarm bells going off in his head. Still, maybe he was wrong and these men had just been put in a bad situation.

Whatever the case, Jacob decided it would be best if he changed out of his pajamas and announced his presence before they bashed down his door. He walked into the back room and changed as quickly as he could into a pair of faded denim jeans, worn thin from years of use, they were his favorite. His wife had once referred to them as his lucky jeans, since he'd never let her throw them out, and that was the only reason she could see for it.

He smiled: Margie had been a hell of a woman. He missed her like crazy these days. He just knew she'd have been right beside him during all this, making it so much more pleasant.

Shaking himself from his memories, he threw on his orange hunting vest. Better that he made himself visible, so he didn't get shot by accident. He also grabbed three packs of cigarettes from the carton he kept in the closet. Jacob wasn't a smoker himself, but he'd gotten them to barter with, should the need arise one day, and he was hoping that it might serve as a peace offering.

Jacob walked to the front door, and opened it. He made eye contact with the one who seemed to be the leader, and held up the cigarettes.

"You boys don't happen to have coffee you could trade for cigarettes now do you?" He asked loudly. Jacob didn't see who pulled the gun, wasn't sure it mattered really. He looked numbly down at his stomach, spraying blood all over the sidewalk. His mouth formed an 'O' of silent surprise and the gun shot rang in his ears. Everything was slow motion, and he felt himself dazedly hoping one of the neighbors was home, would come and help.

He knew no one was though, because he'd checked himself months ago. Still, hope springs eternal in the human mind, and Jacob found himself clinging to it, as his eyes flickered from house to house. He stood there for a moment, almost frozen, almost comically, in horror.

There, his eyes saw the flash of binoculars at the Henderson house, but how? The Henderson's had been on the first evacuation flight. He realized as he fell, it must be his mind playing tricks. No one was coming; no one would ever know what happened to him.

He lay on the hard ground, feeling the life drain from him, dripping steadily onto the sidewalk. He could see the raiders picking up the cigarettes he'd dropped. He sure hoped the Thompson kid was okay. He'd been the one to convince Slade to stay, and he sure as hell hoped the boy had more sense than he did when it came to these men. Jacob's eyes grew heavy, and his breathing shallow. He gurgled, tasting his own blood, and his last thought before the blackness claimed him was 'Margie'.

# Chapter 6

Slade opened his door quickly, and slammed it shut just as fast. "Fuck!" Did he have to slam it?! He was panting from the run, legs shaking beneath his weight. His stomach was roiling, and his mind was whirling in horror at what he'd just witnessed. He hit himself in the head.

"Think, think, think!" He told himself harshly. He'd been smart enough to wait for nightfall before making his mad dash home, praying the raiders hadn't noticed him. He'd watched on in silent, sickening, panic as Andrews had walked out holding up the cigarettes. All the while, he'd been screaming at him in his mind, telling him to get the fuck back in the house!

And then it happened. They'd killed him! The fucking raiders, no murderers, had killed him! Why? What threat could Jacob possibly pose to them? He'd been an old man! Hell, he'd been offering them goddamn cigarettes when the bastards had shot him in cold blood. Then, as he'd stood there, looking for help, Slade could have sworn he'd looked right at him, smiled, and then fallen.

His heart was in his throat, and tears were burning behind his eyes. Slade was fighting them, refusing to cry. He'd never seen death before. He'd sure as hell never seen anyone murdered in cold blood, and sat there, helpless to do anything about it. His stomach heaved, and he swallowed hard, not that he had anything left to throw up, he'd done that already. His eyes were burning worse, and his throat was dry, a lump had formed there, and he wondered if it would ever go away. Panic was welling, and he was shaking all over.

*STOP!* He thought. He didn't have the luxury of crying; he'd shed his tears at the scene, now he needed to focus. He needed to figure his shit out if he was going to get out of here alive. And he sure as hell wasn't going to let them kill him like they'd killed Jacob. He needed to leave. He had no idea when they'd be coming up his street, but he needed to leave.

Slade felt his mind spinning as he tried to concentrate on what to take and what to leave. He could only bring as much as he could carry, and he rapidly ran down the list of necessities: water, food, clothing, sleeping bag, knife, multi-tool. He knew there was more, and when he grabbed his large rucksack that housed his go-bag stuff he was sure he would think of it.

Where would he go? It came to him with such clarity the instant he'd thought the question: 'Mercy Field Campground'. The camp was close by, and home to yurt cabins, they kept firewood year round. He could make it on foot in an hour or two if he hiked quickly.

Having figured out his location, he flew around the house gathering his supplies. His go-bag already contained clothing, a rolled up sleeping bag and a few days of water and food. He decided to cram some more in there along with his crank radio, and the batteries and charger he'd scavenged. His go-bag was a large 5-day survival bag meant for long hikes. It's aluminum back plate, and chest/waist straps meant it could handle more weight without becoming too much of a burden.

Once he'd filled it, he tested it on his back. It was heavy, but do-able. He dropped it by the back door, and took off to grab his fishing vest. It was a black vest with tons of pouches in it that he could use to carry a few more things. He began to put his tools into his fishing vest; multi-tool, folding knife, flash light, binoculars, meal replacement bars and few extra packages of water.

He added the food and water as an after-thought, that way he could eat and drink on the hike if he needed to. Not that he thought he would feel like eating anytime soon. Slade took the vest and put it with the go-bag.

He would leave first thing in the morning, at dawn. The raiders probably wouldn't be up by then, and his body desperately needed rest. He'd wake up in the morning feeling a bit refreshed and take off as fast as he could. Looking around at his house, he had a sinking feeling. He couldn't let the raiders get their hands on his supplies. Those murdering, thieving bastards couldn't be allowed to have it. He would make sure they didn't get to a damn thing.

Slade made his way to the basement. A few summers ago he'd had to replace a support beam, which had broken due to dry rot. He had gotten the section replaced and put in a new support bar to make it more secure. Slade was a man with a plan: he removed the support bar and began to cut away at the support beam until it was almost cut through.

With a few hard swings of an axe he'd managed to knock down the support beam. Slade wiped the sweat from his forehead and climbed the stairs. He still had a lot of work to do before bed.

Slade dragged all of the furniture he could to the right spot in the living room, causing an instant dip in the floor where the support beam was removed. He knew that in the morning when he pushed his fridge over onto it, it would collapse the floor into the basement. His supplies would be hidden, and he could wait for the raiders to move on. Then, when he got hungry, and desperate enough he'd dig them out. He would survive.

# Chapter 7

The alarm clock bleated for about a millisecond before Slade's hand shot out to silence it. He sat upright, a grim look on face. He was ready. He climbed out of bed, and put on his wool socks. He slid up his military style cargo pants. He slid his belt through the loops, putting pouches and tools on as he went. The first was his fixed blade knife with a hammer pommel, then the pouch containing his bear mace, next, his camera pouch. Once it had housed his digital camera, now it was stuffed with a bit of candy.

The last piece of kit he added was another camera pouch. This one was a mirror of some of his other kit: a folding knife, flashlight, and a multi-tool. He had them as a back-up, just in case. He threw on his favorite plaid shirt, and his Algerian style field jacket. He had no idea how long he'd be gone, but he wanted to make sure he would stay warm. He laced up his combat boots, and headed downstairs to gear up.

As he walked down the hallway, he took a hard look at each photo on the wall. He wasn't sure when, or if he'd ever see their faces again, and he wanted to commit them to memory. His mom, her long auburn hair was a curly, frizzy cloud around her head and shoulders. Her smile was broad, loving, and her blue eyes were alight with laughter. He smiled back and ran his hand over her face, feeling sick.

His dad, standing next to his mom, he was tall, broad shouldered. He'd gone grey a few years ago, and he wore an uncomfortable smile. Slade's stomach clenched: he even missed his dad, stony-faced bastard that he was. Slade laughed, thinking of the last time he'd hugged his dad, who'd stood there, stiff and awkward.

Lastly, the photo of Sarah, her long black hair cascading around her, she was pouting slightly. Her eyes were such a dark brown they were almost back, and her lashes were dark and thick. She'd been gorgeous, and he'd really loved her. He ran his hand over her face, tracing her lips. Right before the disaster he'd been shopping for a ring.

Then she was gone, and he had stayed. He'd thought it was only going to be a few weeks at most before she came back, and they'd get married. He pressed a kiss to his fingers, and touched it to the photo. *Love you, Sarah,* he thought fiercely. He was determined to live to see her again.

Slade looked back at them all one last time, and then rushed down the stairs. It was time to get this show on the road. He hoped that his plan worked as he thought it would. He'd hate for nothing to happen after all that work, or hell, for the whole house to collapse on him.

He walked to the edge of the living room. Then, deciding to risk it, he shoved the fridge as hard as he could, sending it flying into the couch. He leapt back, covering his ears and watched his plan work as the floor sagged, held for just a moment, and then the weight caused it to collapse in a loud crash. Slade jogged back to the back door, and threw on his vest and backpack, securing the packs straps.

He walked back to take one last quick look at the hole in the floor. The wood and drywall had nicely covered all of his supplies, concealing them well. He smiled smugly to himself as looked down. He felt bile rise in his throat as he thought about leaving, and tried humor to lighten his mood.

"Insurance!" He laughed, sounding on the edge of panic. He choked the laugh to an end, and walked out his back door, scrambling into the woods at the edge of his yard.

As he passed into the tree line, Slade heard the sound of the trucks coming up his street. His heart was beating a mile a minute as he watched them start up like they had the day before on Inkwell. Was it only yesterday? Had it really been less than 24 hours ago that Jacob had been alive? That he'd been safe in his own home, content with his lot?

To Slade it felt like a lifetime had passed. He was no longer the same man, and he was shocked to discover that he was perversely hopeful one of the raiders would fall into the hole he'd created. He hadn't meant it to be a trap, but the idea of vengeance sure sounded good about now.

Slade forced himself to turn away and move on. He couldn't risk being spotted. Maybe they wouldn't even explore his house, but if they did, he hoped the hole sure made them think twice. It didn't matter. He was alive, and he planned to stay that way the whole trip to Mercy Field Campground and back. Whatever it took, Slade Thompson was going to live, damn it.

# Chapter 8

Slogging through the wet forest was harder than Slade had anticipated. His heavy pack was slowing him down considerably and he was now well into his 4th hour of a trip he'd estimated would take 2 at most. It wasn't yet noon, so he wasn't worried about losing light. It was just that he was getting so tired, and hungry. Not to mention that he wanted to get to Mercy Field to secure his shelter.

Slade let out a gusty sigh as he spotted a large rock, perfect for resting on. He dropped onto it, with his bag still on his back. He reached into one of his camera pouches and pulled out some of the Marshmallow Tammy's he'd packed. The sugary treat was sweet, and delicious. It melted on his tongue, and he savored it as long as he could.

The sound of a twig snapping caused Slade to look up, tilting his head curiously he stared.

"Hunh. That's a big cat." He said to no one in particular. It was then that he noticed the lynx's behavior.

It was stalking towards him, heavy footed, it's element of stealth gone. Slade's eyes widened as he realized what was about to happen. He reached back for his bear spray, but it was under the pack and he couldn't get to it! Adrenaline rushed through his veins and he struggled harder to get it. Even with the adrenaline pumping he couldn't get to it fast enough. The lynx's head went down, the rest of it's body dipping low. It was mere seconds from pouncing.

Slade reached forward, changing tactics, grabbing his knife from its pouch as the cat leapt. It's powerfully muscled body hit hard, and the knife went deep. Hot, wet blood sprayed his face as the cat viciously flailed, trying to claw at him, trying to sink its teeth in. Slade pulled the knife back, and slammed it in again, and again, until the fierce, sleek cat was silent, and lay dead in his lap.

Scrambling backwards, away from the body, Slade gasped like he was drowning. It sure felt like he was. One thing after another, after another. He wiped frantically at the blood on his face, wanting it gone. The spray of blood had reminded him of Jacob, and he couldn't get the image out of his mind.

He slid the knife back into the holster, and forced himself to calm down. Taking deep, cleansing breaths, he slowed his heart rate. *Think of rainbows, and puppies,* he thought, trying for levity. He let out another panic laced laugh, and his shoulders shook, perilously close to shock.

Slade jumped up, and did some jumping jacks. He'd read somewhere once that it could help if you felt you were going into shock. He wasn't sure if it was true or not, all he knew was he needed to do something to get himself together. Something fast. It worked, snapping him out of his horror, and reminding him to go on.

The rest of the hike was uneventful, and a half hour later Slade had found his way to the campground. As he walked onto the grounds, he spotted the pool of water, Mercy Pond. He dropped his pack, and his vest next to the swimming hole, and plunged his hands into the cool water. He scrubbed the blood from his hands and arms, and then went to work on his neck and chest.

The cold water shocked him, but he scrubbed nonetheless, determined to rid himself of the physical reminder of his first kill. After a few more moments of scrubbing, he sat back on his heels, and looked around. *I guess this is my temporary home now.* Slade had lost his friend, lost his house, and killed his first attacking animal in the span of 24 hours. As he stared at the campground hopelessly he wondered if he was doomed to fail? Was it worth it? Could he even do this?

When Slade reached down for more water to clean his face, he caught sight of his reflection. Gone was the face he saw everyday in the mirror, the boy who innocently thought the world would come back in a few weeks. Replacing it was a hardened, blood soaked man. The man who stared back at him looked grim and determined. He was going to fight, to live. He wasn't going to lie down and die. If Slade had needed a sign that he should go on, there was no better one than this. He would survive. He had to.

*****

Watch for **Slade: A Survival Memoir**, coming to a bookstore near you!

# FACT AND FICTION: A SURVIVAL NOVEL

After a disaster that wiped out the East Coast, a vegetarian survivalist fiction writer and his family retire to the shores of a local lake to wait out the anarchy before the relief effort. The fiction he wrote becomes his reality as he relies on his books to give him the knowledge he needs to build, hunt, and survive in this new and foreign world.

Will they survive the oncoming winter?

We never thought that the books that I had collected for my writing career would prove so useful but they would have to save our lives now. I used to write for a survivalist blog and got most of my ideas from books that I had collected from the Internet and army surplus stores and now they were going to be all we had to survive on. Knowledge that was very different than knowledge about how my wife, my daughter and I would have to survive on heavily earmarked books that had made our living for years now. They would make our living in quite a different way now.

It wasn't that America had collapsed, just our little corner of it. With the political landscape being what it was, there was no aid coming our way either and the usual American lifestyle of going to the store and buying groceries every week was obsolete in the Southeastern United States, unless you wanted to drive for three hours away from the coast.

The hurricane that had hit the southeastern coast had destroyed Florida, the death toll was in the tens of thousands and the property damage was in the billions, almost nothing had remained standing. It was the same across the coast pretty much until you reached Virginia. Here in Georgia we had the forest though and we all thought that my collection of survivalist literature would get us through the hard times until reconstruction started so we moved onto the shore of Lake Sinclair and started a new life amid the wreckage of million dollar lakefront homes.

The first task we had was selecting a site to build our new shelter on, something close enough to the water for easy access but not exposed to the cold wind off the lake with winter coming was vital but also from the Boy Scout's handbook I had gotten for a series of child's adventure books I knew that a land depression would be a bad idea too, flooding after rain, deeper snow (on the rare occasion we would get snow), and the fact that cold air would settle lower.

We settled on the far side of a hill from the lake, where the old Bethel Baptist Church had been. They had access to the sewers and if we could get them open we might be able to use them as storage, assuming we could prevent water leakage into them. That first night the three of us huddled together in the car. We had arrived well after sunset and couldn't make even a rudimentary shelter that late so the car seemed safest.

The next morning we all woke up early and started dragging timbers from the church to make a decent shelter, it was still somewhat warm so we had time to work on insulating it a little later, we just needed something to keep us out of the wind and rain. My daughter Sam recommended that we just seal off one end of the overpass but from my reading I knew that was too dangerous because the rain ran right through place. We built a small shelter from roof rafters and chunks of plywood.

I had a vision for a chimney that was rather complicated but would make sure that rain never came though but for now we had a small hut and a grass floor. The floor would need to be improved if this was going to be our long term shelter, it would turn to mud in the rain even if no rain hit it directly and we'd have a lot of problems.

"Tarps!" I said to my wife Elizabeth "We should have brought tarps."

She was confused and asked "Why tarps?"

"They'd make a floor, they make good rain collection in case something should happen to the lake, with enough of them we could entirely waterproof this little shelter and if we should have to move from here they make a decent emergency shelter," I said and she nodded

"Do you think we would have had room for them with all we brought?" She asked.

"We could have made some room I'm sure, anyway, it's too late now. We'll just have to make it without them. We can waterproof the house another way," I said

"How?" She asked, looking pointedly at the gaps in our roof and walls.

"Before asphalt roof tiles people used thatch to make roofs that wouldn't leak, out in the Midwest they covered their roofs with sod back in the Homesteading days. Dirt and grass, they'll make sure we don't get wet," I said with a smile, feeling like all of this was possible.

"I don't know about you but I've seen thatched houses and I'm not seeing anything we're going to do that with here. Everything taller than you or I has been flattened by the damned hurricane. There are some trees left but we can't really get to enough branches to cover this entire thing," she said and I deflated a little bit.

Samantha came to my rescue and said, "We'll waterproof it the same way Africans waterproof their mud huts, enough branches to keep the mud from falling through the roof and then just cover the branches in a thick coating of this thick Georgia clay we can't escape from. It will do the job just fine until we can start pulling bits of these destroyed roofs apart to scavenge shingles. We may want to coat the entire thing in mud before winter. It will help us insulate it. We'll need a chimney so we can make a fire inside before winter comes too."

"How do you know that Samantha?" I asked, surprised.

"Because well you were collecting those books for work I was reading them so that I could go out and be out in the wilderness. I was going to join the Peace Corps before all of this happened and I thought some knowledge of how to survive in the harsher parts of the world would be good for me," she said and I was very surprised, my daughter taking an interest in other parts of the world and being willing to leave home for two years to help them. I walked over and gave her a big hug.

"Thank you, sweetheart. Any other advice for your two doddering old parents?"

She rolled her eyes and said "Yes, our supply of food isn't going to last very long. We need to see about finding somewhere that we can get some more. It's too late in the year to really gather much in the way of plants but there are fish in the river and deer and turkeys in what's left of the woods, a few bears even most likely. Come spring if we follow bear tracks they're likely to lead us to good fishing spots. I don't know about you two but I know I've never been fishing or hunting so we're going to have to figure that out together."

"I have a book on traps and snares. Maybe we can rig some up for the local wildlife," I said, rather disgusted at the thought that I was going to have to kill an animal to survive out here. It was an uncomfortable thought to me but I knew I would have to get used to it. I pulled several books out of the bag and passed one to my daughter.

"We can do this if we want to. It beats trying to scramble for the limited supplies in the city. There's never enough there after the floods came through," she said.

My wife nodded and added "She's right, you know. I know you're too gentle to ever be comfortable with doing this but we'll get through it together. We have no choice but to make sure we eat with the winter coming."

"I know Elizabeth, but I don't have to like it. We'll need to use our salt to cure the meat and get some of these hardwood trees down to smoke it," I said and went to the car as much to get a few supplies as to get away from the situation.

This was going to be a hard winter for me and I knew it but I could brace myself and get through it. I came back with two unused fishing poles and handed one to my wife who had been fishing a few times a few years ago for a business trip and that made her the resident expert. She helped me spool the fishing line and attach a lure and bobber, which was just a piece of cork and we walked a few hundred feet to the bank of the lake and looked for a good spot to cast our lines.

There was a school of small fish that I pointed out to Elizabeth, who said, "If I remember right, we want to cast there because the little fish will attract the bigger ones and those are the ones we really need. Remember though that there's more to fishing than just reeling in the line once you've caught something. Set the drag to about a quarter of your line strength and attach your bait."

She quickly showed me how when I got confused and frustrated and I took a mental note of it so I wouldn't forget. "Now throw your line. When you catch something you want to shorten the line by using the rod, not the reel. Lift the rod then reel in the slack," she said and we cast our lines

"In normal circumstances, this would be relaxing," I said. She laughed a little and then I jumped at a tug on my line. She took the rod from me to show me how it was done the first time. She raised the rod nearly vertically and as she lowered it she would reel in the line and bring the fish closer. After doing this several times the fish was close enough to touch. She reached out with her left hand and grabbed the fish by the head, moving her hand down the body.

"Be careful never to go against the direction of the scales. The fins will spear you," she said and I made a mental note of that as well. She brought it onto the bank pulled out her knife. I turned away as she quickly killed and gutted the fish.

"They suffer less if you do it quickly. You don't want them to suffocate to death," she mentioned and I nodded. I was fixated by the blood on her hands and couldn't turn away.

She handed me the rod and I cast it out into the water again. I was standing there a few minutes when the line jerked again and I mimicked the motions that Elizabeth showed me moments before, the fish struggled harder than the one that she had caught but it was soon close enough to be visible, it was a carp about two feet long. I pulled it's head out of the water like I was shown and with a trembling hand I cut the fish's head off. I picked the fish up and put it on the bank with the other one.

My wife smiled at me and said, "I told you that you could do it."

I nodded slowly. "I think we have enough for tonight and tomorrow. These are some large fish."

She nodded and said, "I wonder what Samantha's doing."

"Probably being more useful than I am, whatever it is she's doing," I answered.

And indeed the girl was being very useful. She came back to our little shelter (I refused to call it a home at this point in our residency) with a heaping bundle of plants in her arms.

"What are these?" My wife asked

"Food," Samantha said with a smile "Cattail, clover, dandelion, wild onion, some violets and chickweed too. I see you two caught some fish so we'll be able to eat quite well tonight."

She put the food on a piece of stainless steel that we had salvaged from the church and took the fish from her mother before saying to me, "Why don't you go get us some water so I can boil these cattail and dandelion roots and we'll have something like fish and mashed potatoes for dinner, just like at home."

That touch of confidence in her voice was enough to shake me out of the daze I was in from killing my first fish and I grabbed the larger of the two pots we had brought with us and went to the lake to fill it with water.

When I got back, Samantha was reading one of my unfinished essays. She looked up and said, "How is it that you know all this on paper and have never done any of it?"

"How is it you know how the Revolutionary War was fought but have never done it?" I pointed to the stack of books she was sitting next to. "Those books, they are all I know about surviving out here and I never felt the need to remember it, only to bookmark it in case I needed it later."

She laughed at that, saying, "This is important stuff, Dad. I understand why you never took me camping though. I mean the look on your face when you came in with mom and those fish, priceless, absolutely priceless. If I had had a camera at that moment."

She grabbed the Audubon Society Field Guide to Southeastern Plants and tossed it at me.

"You can gather plants though, at least until you get used to this. You've been a vegetarian too long to have you go around catching and killing your own food just yet. Let the hamburger eaters get our hands dirty until you feel capable."

I nodded and moved closer to hug her and she continued, "We'll get through this, Dad, trust me. I know this isn't exactly what you, as an envirofreak, vegetarian, artist wanted, but it's the best way to get through until we get a decent relief effort and not the pathetic job this country in shambles is doing now."

I hugged her tight. I was proud of her. One of the things I had wanted for her was that she be a stronger, better person than I was and this was proof of that. Tears flowed from my eyes and I wiped them off with my sleeve before releasing her.

Elizabeth returned from the car with a cast-iron pan and said, "I need you two to go out and find me something to cook over. I mean having a fire is all well and good but how am I supposed to cook so-called potatoes and grill fish if I don't have something resembling a stove? Go find me something, even a slab of rock will be fine if we can prop it up with the bricks from the house down the hill."

Sam and I stepped out of our shelter and walked towards the house that had the bricks. "We'll have to pull some of those bricks out to make an oven sometime during the winter. Bricks or something else that would radiate heat longer than a fire alone will reduce our fuel consumption during the worst of the cold."

"Where did you learn all this anyway?" I asked her, still somewhat shocked.

"Do you remember Tyler?" She asked, blushing a little

"Tyler, wasn't that the boy, two years ago? A little strange, took you.... mudding was it?"

She laughed, "Yes, that Tyler. And unknown to you, he took me camping several times as well. I told you that I was sleeping over at Kayla's but mom knew." She laughed even louder at my shocked face and then said, "Don't worry, nothing happened. Anyway, I wanted to impress him by knowing something about how to take care of myself out in the woods so I borrowed your books a few times. We actually camped about a half mile from here."

She pointed out across the lake to what had been a small campground.

"Right there. He tried to get me to sleep with him there but I was totally not interested. He was VERY drunk. I wasn't. Though he did bring wine coolers to try and get me that way but I brought them home and gave them to Christina."

I marveled at all of this new knowledge that was being given to me by my beloved Samantha. I pointed out the top grate to an old Weber grill, the rest of it had been flung to another place by the wind but the grate was sitting there, looking rusted and forlorn.

"Will that work?" I asked.

"It could but something bigger would be better. There were large charcoal grills over in that campsite that have something the size we'd ne- OW!" She jumped up and down holding her foot and I looked down to see that she had kicked a large slab of rock that was buried under some leaves.

"Or we could use that," she said after she had recovered herself and uttered a lot of words I would usually have scolded her for saying.

Between the two of us, we lifted the slab of rock and carried it back to Elizabeth, who directed us where to set it down and then sent us scurrying for bricks to prop it up so she could make a fire under it. Sam and I returned with an armload of bricks each and we quickly arranged a small cooking stove out of them. We pulled out some of the kindling and wood that we had all gathered in the morning and Elizabeth and I quickly got to work cooking while our daughter sat down and read.

We had brought far too many books with us but it was the only way that we were all going to keep our sanity being alone out here for as long as we thought we would be. I had also packed something secret that I would bring out when we were running out of reading material.

Samantha poked her head over my shoulder and said, "It smells good. Did you cut up some of the wild onion to add to the roots?"

"Yes," I said as I watched my wife flip the carp filets. She had cut them off with more grace than I expected and the meat was turning from translucent red to opaque pink on the skin side. I was fascinated by the fact that this fish had been flapping in my hands barely three hours ago and here parts of it were in a black pan.

I had to admit that it smelled good, even though the thought of eating a living creature still seemed uncomfortable to me but I knew that I had no choice if I wanted to survive this winter, there wasn't going to be any protein available if I didn't eat this fish and many more like it. My wife served the fish on our white plastic plates that had seen better days; they had cuts in them and were stained with spaghetti sauce from a hundred dinners.

I tentatively took a bite and chewed slowly. Samantha was eating very quickly, having worked up an appetite over the course of the day. My wife was watching me carefully over her plate. I swallowed the bite of fish and took a bite of the mashed roots - they were very good. The fish was very good, too. That much I had to admit.

"What do you think?" Elizabeth asked.

"I think I'll be able to eat out here," I said and took another small bite of the fish. "I think we need to pull out our seeds in the spring though, this needs herbs."

"We can plant them here and now if we get a window. The fire will keep them warm enough that they don't freeze," Sam said, "The trick will be finding a window that isn't smashed."

"What if we were to grow them on the roof? Plant it with sod like they did out in the mid-west and grow them there. We'll keep the place warm enough that the ground above us shouldn't freeze. We have a fish for tomorrow so we can all spend the day putting sod on as a roof," I said.

"That could work," Elizabeth answered. Soon, tired from the day, we all went to sleep, planning to improve our little dwelling tomorrow.

We all woke up in the middle of the night shivering. The fire had gone out. I began to swear, dearly missing our central heating, or at least electric space heaters and then Sam and I got to work starting the fire again, we searched in the dark for more kindling and lit it with one of our lighters before carefully adding larger and denser pieces of wood to the fire.

This time I sat up and watched the fire until sunrise, all the while wondering if we had made the right decision to come out here and live on the lake like we were. This was not our environment and where Sam was adapting well and Elizabeth seemed reasonably comfortable I wasn't sure if I could ever get used to this life. Sunrise came quickly though and I woke them up to start the day's project.

We all got up and put on our coats and I had the passing thought that our reasonably light weight clothes would not last very long under the strain we were going to put them under in the next few months. It was worth considering how to replace them now before it became a crisis.

Apparently sodding a roof is more complicated than just digging up chunks of grass and dirt and affixing them between the holes in your roof. We tried that for about two hours and bits of dirt would fall down into our structure even without the additional burden of rain and wind, we needed a new technique.

This wasn't something I had a book on though, most of my books were short-term survival not go out and make a new life in the forest. I knew that the plywood would keep us dry for a few months at least but we knew we needed something that would keep us dry in the long term and not suffer from water damage and rot over the course of a wet winter and spring, we also needed something to block the holes and cracks in the plywood.

"We need something solid to fill up those holes before we put the sod over the roof," I said

"No duh, Dad," Sam said with frustration "But what do we use?" She kicked a tree in annoyance and then our faces all brightened. "Tree bark!" She said

"But doesn't tree bark rot faster than plywood?" I said.

"Birch bark is waterproof," Elizabeth exclaimed "I learned that in my Asian history class. The Mongols would make cases for their bows out of birch bark. You can also cut birch bark off without killing the tree."

"Well, let's go find some!" I said, very excited. I quickly ran inside to get the Audubon field guide so we could know what we were looking for. It had peeling cinnamon colored bark so we all set out together in search of one with Samantha in charge of our compass so we didn't get lost and could find our way back after we got the bark we needed.

We found a few of them surprisingly quickly and peeled off as much of the outer bark as we could reach and carry, being careful not to pull off the inner bark in case we needed the trees later in the winter to patch a hole. I took it in my hands and thought that I could write on it if I needed to and that was a comforting thought. I needed something to write on if we were going to be here long.

I pulled off a piece of the inner bark and put it in my mouth without thinking. "Hey this seems edible!" I said as I swallowed it

"Dad! You didn't! Don't eat anything in the woods that you don't know is safe, the plants could kill you if you eat them." Sam yelled

I spat the remains out of my mouth and cursed my carelessness. We rushed home to check the edible plants book we had to see if I was in for a very unpleasant evening, carrying armfuls of birch bark home with us. I opened the book and checked on birch trees.

"We're going to be okay. It was actually a common Native American food source during harsh winters. The leaves are edible too, and the sap can be boiled and is sweet like maple syrup."

"You were lucky. Don't do it again," Elizabeth said.

I nodded and said "Yes, dear. I know it was stupid but I just wasn't thinking. I usually put things in my mouth that don't belong there. I like to chew on things."

"We'll have to find you something safe to chew on then," she said and we all went back outside to put the bark on the roof.

The sod went on much easier then, well it didn't go on any easier but it didn't fall into our shelter with the birch bark plugging the holes. We were sure to leave a small hole above where we made our fires so the smoke would clear. It was almost sunset when the last of the dirt and grass went on to our small hut. I could hardly imagine what it would take to sod an entire home and respected my ancestors for doing so.

My wife showed me how to filet a fish and I didn't react as badly as I thought I would, she had me cook it this time and I also wilted some of the kudzu leaves down and cooked them like I would spinach. I had a moment of pride as we ate. Everything on the plates was gathered and prepared by my little family. It was a small victory but it was a victory nonetheless.

"Tomorrow we'll plant the herbs on the roof," Elizabeth said and Sam nodded without looking up from her book.

She was about a quarter of the way through On the Road by Jack Kerouac, it was one of my favorites at her age and I would have to ask her what she thought about it while we worked tomorrow. Tonight I just wanted to sleep, sodding the roof had been more physically demanding work than I had done in more than a decade and there wasn't even a hot shower to clean myself in, just a freezing cold lake. We piled the fire high before going to sleep and made sure that everything flammable was out of the range of sparks.

"We'll need to make something to cover that hole from the rain without stopping air from passing through it before too long," I said as I laid my head down on one of the last true comforts of home, my very comfortable pillow and down comforter. The girls muttered their responses at me as we all fell into a well deserved sleep.

I was the last to awake and there was already a bustle of activity around me in the cold October morning. The girls were carrying bricks from the remains of the church into the shelter and I quickly put my clothes on and joined them, wondering what they were for. We had a stack of nearly two hundred bricks when Sam and Elizabeth started sweeping the remains of the fire out the door and then started laying bricks where the fire had been.

"We're building an oven, basically," Elizabeth said. We heat the bricks and the bricks keep us warm while we sleep. We can even take some hot bricks and put them in water for a bath if we ever find something that will serve as a tub."

We laid two layers of bricks on the ground and then made a wall of bricks to contain the fire that was three layers thick and almost two feet high. We placed the rock slab that we were using as a stove over one side so that we could easily add fuel to the fire without taking the slab off every time. It was almost noon when we were done laying the bricks and then we went out into the wood to gather more plants for dinner.

"We need to make a carrying basket," Sam said. "We can lift more than we can carry in our arms or even in my backpack."

"We'll have to work on it," I said as we started yanking at the kudzu that had ruined one of the houses. On the other hand it was the only house still standing. That thought amused me and then it occurred to me "This house is still standing!" I shouted.

"Yeah, so what?" Samantha said.

"So... what could we salvage from it?" I answered.

"I don't know - I'm afraid it will collapse at any moment."
Elizabeth said warily.

"Dear, this house is the only one for miles to survive a
hurricane." I said

"Yes but the kudzu has torn more into its structure since then.
I've seen houses overrun by vines. I don't trust them." She
continued.

Samantha felt none of my wife's misgivings and was already
through the weatherworn door and looking through the house.

"Hey. Someone lived here at one point!" she called out through
the door. "There are signs of squatters."

I went in and Elizabeth hesitantly followed. There were signs of
life here, life hastily abandoned. Whoever bought this million-
dollar house hadn't lived here in years but there had been an
occupant after them. I desperately wished to be able to flick on
some lights and see what I was doing but there was no power of
course. We found a small pile of blankets in the corner. They
were dry and Samantha picked them up, folded them and put
them by the door so we could leave with them. We continued to
search to the house.

I gasped and smiled. "Tarps!" I exclaimed, "It's our lucky day!"

I took a step forward and my leg fell through a weak spot in the floor where it had been water damaged. I caught myself and lifted my leg out of the hole, wincing at the blood that was dripping down my leg.

"Let's finish the search and then we can go get my leg bandaged. There are too many valuable things here," I said and they nodded.

We continued to search the large house there wasn't much more other than a few cans that would provide us with food for a few days but would have to be reserved as an emergency food supply. As we were leaving Sam noticed a small bag tucked into the corner and picked it up and we walked away with our tarps, blankets, and cans. I limped a little as we walked back to our shelter. We climbed into our house and I limped over to the stocked first-aid bag that we had known we would need. I got the tweezers and some rubbing alcohol.

"Sam. I need you to pull the splinters out of my leg and then clean the wounds with rubbing alcohol. We'll bandage it when you're done. Elizabeth got to folding the blankets and laid another one on each of our bedrolls. There were ten blankets and I smiled as I looked at the solid black tarps. The smile was quickly wiped from my face as Sam smeared the rubbing alcohol on my leg. I winced and tightened my hands into fists.

"Why are you so happy about the tarps?" Elizabeth asked

"Well for one, do you remember when we were talking about hot baths? You can make a bathtub with a tarp and a frame. Drop some of our hot bricks in it and we have warm water," I said

Sam pulled another splinter out of my leg and wiped the swab of alcohol over my leg causing me to wince again.

A few moments later all the splinters were out of my leg and it was wrapped it white gauze. They left me resting in our shelter and went out to get a fish for dinner. I picked up one of the dozens of survival books we had brought along and started reading it. It was a book on trapping small game and I knew that that was the next step in providing food for the winter.

Rabbits, birds, perhaps even snakes and squirrels. I knew that squirrels would be something I wouldn't have as strong objections to eating. I had been attacked by a squirrel in my youth and still had some resentment towards the squeaking tree rats. I knew about rabbit starvation and I was almost certain that applied to squirrels as well so we would need some form of fat to survive.

For a brief moment, I was consumed by the thought that this was impossible and we were only delaying our inevitable deaths from starvation and exposure out here but I quickly banished the thought. Everything we do is only delaying our inevitable deaths. Death comes to all of us. The important thing is to do what you can with the time you have. I read this book about traps and hoped that it all was as easy as this book made it seem.

After I had read through the relevant sections, I picked up the edible plants guide and turned it back to the birch tree. We needed a spile to get into the tree and extract the sap. I knew what one was supposed to look like so we could make one if we had the materials. It would be nice to have something sweet out here; a little taste of home would make this experience a bit more bearable.

Samantha and Elizabeth came back with a large fish and Elizabeth showed me how to scale and filet a fish. She did one side and I horribly butchered the other side in my attempt to mimic her motions. The scaling was reasonably easy but the fileting was more than I could figure out the first time. She took the torn chunks of fish that I had cut and cut them into even pieces to cook.

I felt that this meal was missing bread of some variety but that was a dream that would never be fulfilled. Where would we find flour and yeast to make bread here? We ate just the fish tonight as we had been too busy retrieving things from the standing house to gather plants to eat.

"Soon there will be no plants to eat," I said after a bite of fish.

"We'll have to eat something plant-based. Scurvy and all that. You can't avoid scurvy without plants," Elizabeth said.

"It seems so strange to be talking about scurvy. What is this, the 18th century?" Sam commented through a mouthful of food. I couldn't help but agree with her, we were in a shelter that was smaller than some rooms, with no power, and worrying about diseases that had been eliminated over a century ago. This was not what I had signed up for when we started this journey.

"Yes, but it will all be over soon enough. We just have to stay safe out here while people get funding to rebuild," Elizabeth said

"And then we'll come home to find our house destroyed and looted," I said bitterly. It was hard to keep myself from being upset by this situation. It seemed the world was against us right now and that all we could do was hide and do our best to live through it. We had been a comfortable family, better off than some and now we were sitting in a hovel and trying to figure out how we would survive.

Elizabeth saw the upset look on my face and said, "It will all be alright. We'll do just fine here. By the spring you'll feel just as comfortable here as you ever did at home."

"Assuming we survive the winter," I said

"We're in Georgia. It's not like the winters here are terribly deadly. It doesn't even snow every year. The lake won't even freeze," she answered. She was from New England and knew exactly what a harsh winter was; she had been snowed in her house for weeks before without power or heat. Sam and I had never gone more than two days without power though and this adjustment was hard.

"I guess we will feel just as at home here," Sam said, "I'm just happy not having to worry about all the high school drama honestly. Nobody cares who's dating who or if I wore the same shirt as one of the vapid cheerleader twits out here. It's refreshing. The only problem will be when I run out of books to read."

I thought back to the secret things I had packed and smiled. There would be nothing to worry about with running out of things to read or do. We cleaned off our plates by dipping them in boiling water and Sam and Elizabeth both picked up their books. I stood up and went outside into the cold. I needed a moment alone with the outside world. I had not been alone out here yet. I looked up at the moon; it was full and brighter than I could remember seeing it in a long time. There were more stars too.

"That is something good about this place," I said and walked down to the lake.

I paced back and forth along the lakeshore for nearly twenty minutes, shivering a bit but trying to come to peace with this reality. I needed to keep it together if only so that I didn't bring the girls down. The cuts on my leg hurt a little bit but not as badly as the alcohol had. I sat down by the lake and splashed some of the cold water onto my face.

This would be okay. It had to be okay. I wiped my face off on my sweater sleeve and went back inside. I didn't feel like I had achieved a lasting peace with this but I was okay for the moment. I picked up Finnegan's Wake when I came inside and started to read with the rest of my family.

*****

Several weeks went by of eating plants that Sam identified and whatever fish we could pull out of the lake when I decided to secretly set my first traps. We needed something other than fish in our diet and I was hoping that I could find something. I had been reading everything we had brought with us on trapping small animals for nearly three weeks and felt confident that I could set something. It occurred to me as I felt this confidence that I wasn't as squeamish about killing things to survive any more.

I decided to start with my old enemy the squirrel and set up a squirrel pole against some nearby trees. The pole was propped at a 45 degree angle against the tree and I placed several wire nooses going up and down the pole, about two inches from touching the poles. The theory was that a curious squirrel would climb up the pole and get caught in one of the nooses, it would then struggle to get out and fall off the pole and then we had dinner.

If I was lucky, I could get several squirrels with the same trap. I also made a couple of bottle holes. Digging out a hole where the bottom of the hole was wider than the top of the hole so that the walls were angled inward. I then covered it with an elevated piece of wood. Mice and other small skittish creatures would run under the concealing wood and get trapped in the hole because they can't climb up the backwards-angled walls.

They weren't much but they would give us a starting place for things. Even if we just used the catches from these to bait a larger trap it was something. I was sure to cover my scent as the book taught me, rubbing down my hands with rotted vegetation so that the scent of human wouldn't be on the traps.

I walked back to the shelter to find the girls still asleep and grabbed the backpack and the edible plants book to try and get a head start on gathering food for the grand meal I had planned. I had built a spile in secret over the past few days and left it in one of the birch trees back out in the forest.

This was a big thing that I was hoping would all work out well and I would have a surprise for my wife and daughter. I walked back to my tapped birch tree and found nearly two gallons of sap in the bucket I hung off of my improvised spile. I was thrilled to see the liquid in the bucket. I had not expected this few inches of copper pipe to actually draw sap from a tree but here it was. I poured the contents of the bucket into two large water bottles and hung the bucket back under the tree.

This was another of the victories that seemed so rare to me, this was not my world but I was surviving here with help. I pulled some kudzu leaves, cattail roots and dandelions. This would be the greatest success I'd had in this forest. I was beginning to look forward to more of them; I had grown to become somewhat hopeful that we would survive the winter.

I came back to the shelter to find the girls out doing something and I hid my finds under my blanket to surprise them when they came back. I went out to check one of my squirrel poles and found two large squirrels dangling from the pole. I jumped with joy and went to retrieve my prizes, making sure to reset the snare as I left. Flushed with my success I went to check the bottle holes I had dug and found some of them to have mice in them.

I quickly and mercifully crushed their skulls before putting them in my bag. The last one I came to had a snake inside it with half of the mouse that had hidden inside in its mouth. I took advantage of my good fortune and crushed the snake's skull as I would a mouse and put it in my bag. The final tally of my traps was two squirrels, four mice, and a snake. I wasn't sure what I'd do with the meal that I was carrying home but I knew we'd have a feast compared to our usual diet of fish.

The fish were plentiful but it was getting very tiring eating the same thing again and again. Our herb garden was being kept warm enough by the heat from our fires to grow though and we were seeing sprouts so soon we would be able to season our meat.

When I came back the last time it was getting to about five o'clock. The sun was just dipping behind the trees. The girls were waiting for me.

Samantha asked, "Where have you been all day?"

I hugged her and answered "Here and there. Being a general nuisance to every living thing within a mile."

Elizabeth laughed and said "Should we all go get a fish for dinner? Sam and I gathered up some more edible plants. We found a patch of wild violet and sorrel today. We're going to spend tomorrow transplanting some of it closer to us."

I pretended to whine, "I'm not in the mood for fish. We need something else."

"Well, what do you have in mind, Dad? I don't see any other animals parading by for us to eat them." Sam said sarcastically

"You clearly haven't been looking very hard," I said and I pulled one of the squirrels out of my bag. "I set some traps this morning before you all woke up and checked them when you were out gathering plants. I have a fair bit of meat here."

Sam and Elizabeth were shocked, and both hugged me tight.

"That's not the only surprise I have. Do you remember how the book said that birch sap was like maple sap?" I said, pleased to see them so excited

"Yes," They both replied.

I uncovered my bottle of birch sap and said, "I've spent a few days working on a spile. That's what you use to extract sap from a tree. This is my first harvest." I took a small sip and said, "It tastes like sweet grass mixed up in water."

They beamed with excitement as I laid it all out before them

"Hun, I never thought you'd do so well at this," Elizabeth said.

"Yeah, Dad, I'm really proud of you," Samantha said as she took a sip of the birch sap "This is good!" She smiled and handed it to her mother.

I almost felt that it was time to bring out the last surprise from home but I wanted to save that to bring a bit of light to the usual hopelessness of deep winter. It was late December and we usually all had a patch of blackness in January. It could wait until then.

We all worked together to skin my catches and Sam and Elizabeth debated on how to cook them. As they talked I sat down with Finnegan's Wake again and let the joy wash over me.

This wasn't long-term survival but any moment of joy is a moment to be savored. I let Joyce's words flow through me. *Yasha Yash ate sassage and mash. So found he bash, poor Yasha Yash.*

We decided to roast the mice on sticks and hang the squirrels and snake outside so they would keep until tomorrow when we would make squirrel soup and sauté the snake stuffed with leaves. Sam cooked the mice and we made mashed roots, dripping the fat from the rats into the mash to make it creamier. We all sat down to it with a glass of birch sap and had the best meal we had had so far on this adventure. We all settled down to bed that night with a renewed sense of optimism and big plans for the next day.

*****

We woke long after sunrise and brought the snake and squirrels inside. We all went out to look more around in our new local area; we walked back towards where we had left the car. A large parking lot in front of a grocery that had been looted within weeks of the disaster happening. There was nothing inside it but the lot that was in front of it was a good place to leave the car.

Close enough to the shelter that we could reach it if we needed to return to what little civilization there was left here. We would have to go out into the world to gather more supplies but so far we were doing well enough out here. We weren't dead yet at least and that was something. There were several small clusters of edible plants that we marked to transplant closer to our house when we came back.

"We need to get some yeast," I said. "It would be so useful to have around the shelter. I know how to culture yeast but I need yeast to culture first."

Elizabeth nodded and said "We'll be sure to get some when we go back for other supplies. It's not worth going and making a special trip for."

I reluctantly agreed. The temptation to make beer and bread was immense and I was hoping that we would go soon to gather back-up supplies. We'd more first aid supplies eventually though and that would be the perfect opportunity to get what I needed for the comforts of home.

We returned to the shelter and I opened a book on brewing and fermenting and noticed a footnote in the corner that was included as a historical note. *Before the days of packeted brewer's yeast people would forage in the forest for yeast, often the form of white powder on spring and summer berries. The earliest wines were accidentally fermented by wild yeast on the berries.*

This was the miracle I had been searching for. Yeast would be available by spring though there was no way I would find it before the beginning of March when the first buds of flowers started forming here. It was still a glimmer of hope that we could survive in wild without the intervention of the "civilized world" and that that was something I had not expected to find.

I dug through my other books to see if there was any way I could find yeast earlier than spring and though I couldn't find what plants wild yeast grew on I found a description for it. A fine white powder appearing on a plant. Of course I would have to be careful not to ingest a hazardous mold or fungus but if I allowed my yeast to culture before using it I could be sure it was yeast and not something dangerous.

Sam apparently saw the excitement on my face as she looked up from her second reading of On the Road "What did you find in that book Dad? You know you can't do anything with it until we go into the city for yeast. Why tease yourself with all the recipes."

I stood up showed her the book, pointing to the footnote about wild yeast. "Dad, you know that aspens have white powder on them a lot right? I'm not sure if it's what you're looking for but they do sometimes have it," I started at the news and said, "Are there any aspens around here?"

I was thrilled about the news and hoped that there would be an aspen local to us. "There aren't any that I've seen here but they do grow here according to the Audubon book. Maybe we'll go look for one after we check your traps and tree tomorrow," Sam said "But for now we've got cooking to do."

We skinned the snake that would serve as the main course tonight and split it down the middle. We stuffed the middle with some of the herbs from our roof. Mostly thyme. We threw some sprigs of thyme on the fire as well to add a sweet smelling smoke to the air. The squirrels were more difficult to skin. We broke the bones to release the marrow into our soup and let it cook with some sorrel and dandelion roots we had gathered yesterday.

"It will almost be like chicken soup with potatoes," I said, having no idea how it would actually taste. I had never tasted squirrel and wondered what it would be like. The soup wouldn't be great, but it would be like the soup that Samwise made for Frodo in Ithillian. I laughed at myself for drawing that conclusion but it seemed true enough to me. Squirrel broth basically would be what it was and that was enough for me to feel better about things. We put the stuffed snake in a low part of the fire to let it sort of bake and boiled the squirrels and roots.

Elizabeth relaxed with a book as Sam and I cooked this little meal. It was nearly an hour before the food was done the way we wanted it. We carefully retrieved the snake from the fire with a forked stick and dispensed the soup into our bowls. The squirrel meat was very tender and tasted a lot like pheasant, which I had had a few times in my youth. It tasted a lot like I remembered that. The snake was more chickeny but in basic analysis a lot of things taste like chicken.

It wasn't quite chicken but it could have been used in most of the same recipes, which was a good thing for our future cooking with herbs here. We ate well and then sat around the fire talking. Sam told her mother about our plan to go harvest wild yeast when we could and Elizabeth smiled and nodded indulgently. She wasn't thrilled about the idea of eating things we were uncertain of but she wouldn't complain so long as I was safe about it.

We took the leftovers of the remains of the meat about a mile away from our shelter and buried them. We didn't want to attract any predators or scavengers to our part of the forest but we also needed to dispose of it before it rotted.

I awoke early the next day, very excited about the possibility of finding yeast for us as well as checking my traps again to see if they had brought us anything fresh in the day since I had been out to check them. Sam woke earlier than she would have liked, slowly pulled out of sleep by the sound of me pacing back and forth in our house.

We went out to check the tapped birch tree first and found nearly another gallon of liquid waiting in the bucket. We quickly put it into the bottles we had brought for the purpose and went on to the traps. Squirrels were plentiful on the poles. Between the ten poles I had set up two days ago there were six squirrels. The bottle traps were empty though and I resolved to bait them next time, maybe bait them to catch snakes instead of mice.

We walked deeper into the forest. We had walked nearly until noon and were turning back when we realized that we had gotten lost. We knew we had headed roughly west as the sun was at our backs the entire time we walked so we turned around and walked back towards the west, hoping we would come to familiar forest.

Two hours later we were still lost and I was beginning to get worried about how to find shelter through the night in case we didn't make it back before sunset. I told Sam this and she laughed a little bit at me. There was no food around other than the squirrels in my bag and we had grown complacent and didn't bring a fire starter with us.

I was genuinely afraid, more afraid than I had been in nearly a month and then it hit me that I had grown accustomed to living in our little patch of forest. Another two hours of walking later and we were still out of sight of land we recognized.

"We should set up camp and settle down for the night," I said "We don't want to take the risk of being caught out here after dark unsheltered"

Sam laughed and said "Dad, if it will make you feel better we can build a shelter and settle down for the night but I'm sure familiar surroundings are just over the next hill."

"I'll give it one more hour," I said "But when the sun starts to set we need to build something." I looked up at the gloomy sky, worried about it raining or even snowing.

Sam smiled and said, "That's the spirit. We'll be home soon enough."

But still another hour passed of going roughly west and we were still lost. Things were beginning to look somewhat familiar but it could just be my desperation to be home. I thought I had seen this tree or that rock before but I didn't know where that was in relation to home.

Sam finally relented and we started gathering material for a shelter. We set up a central pole for a shelter in the fork of a three-trunked tree and began to work as quickly as we could. Grabbing every branch we could find and breaking some off of the nearby trees we built an a-frame shelter but we both knew it wasn't insulated enough.

We started scrambling with our hands to pile loose earth onto this thing but it wasn't working fast enough. We cleared the entire area of loam to insulate our shelter and it was still only a few inches thick instead of the at least a foot we would need to stay warm enough tonight. We walked back the way we came from being lost and dragged small fallen trees towards the shelter hoping to use them as walls so we could pile our limited insulation into a smaller space.

The sunset and we were nowhere near complete with this thing but it was the best we could do, we couldn't work at night. Sam and I crawled in and hoped that our conjoined body heat would keep us warm.

"I'm sorry, Dad," she said. "I should have listened earlier"

"No dear, you were optimistic. It makes sense. It didn't feel like we had walked all that far, the shelter should have been just through the next few trees for hours. We must have been walking at an angle to forest we knew," I said, stroking her hair and making promises to any supernatural being that would listen that if we survived this I would do anything they asked.

It quickly grew cold as night fell and I was sitting here in a space so small I could feel the walls closing in around me as Samantha and I were covered in our coats as improvised blankets and clinging to each other for warmth. I struggled to control my breathing as panic overtook me in the small space. I couldn't show fear, if I panicked she would panic and there was no sense in both of us dying afraid.

It could have been minutes or hours later that the rain started, I lost all track of time in that hole all I knew is that I was colder than I had ever been and felt like I had built my own coffin. I wondered if Elizabeth would ever find us and if she would survive out here without us or drive back into the devastated cities and eek out a living for the foreseeable future. Our teeth were chattering and I knew that I would never take the warmth of a fire for granted again, assuming I survived to feel another one.

"Dad?" She said "Are we g-g-g-oing to die out here?"

I tried to be brave, I tried to say "No" but it came out "I don't know."

So we huddled there in that little thing I couldn't even call a shelter in fairness and she fell asleep. I was too consumed with thoughts of my own mortality and the idea that I was laying in something the size and shape of a coffin. Now was not the best time for claustrophobia but now was the time I felt like I was developing. I wanted more than anything to be away from here.

For the first time, my thoughts didn't whisk me away to our comfortable house in the city but to the little shelter, the little home we had built in the woods here. The one that I would be more pleased than I had ever been in my life to see anything if I could see it again.

"I love you, Sam," I said.

It was these with these words, words that may have been my last, that I finally fell asleep, trembling with cold and wondering if I would ever wake to see the dawn.

*****

Watch for **Fact and Fiction: A Post-Apocalyptic Memoir**, coming to a bookstore near you!

www.ingramcontent.com/pod-product-compliance
Lightning Source LLC
Chambersburg PA
CBHW071409280526
45787CB00001B/500